I0427873

[H.A.S.C. No. 113–131]

THE ROLE OF MARITIME AND AIR POWER IN DOD'S THIRD OFFSET STRATEGY

HEARING

BEFORE THE

SUBCOMMITTEE ON SEAPOWER AND PROJECTION FORCES

OF THE

COMMITTEE ON ARMED SERVICES HOUSE OF REPRESENTATIVES

ONE HUNDRED THIRTEENTH CONGRESS

SECOND SESSION

HEARING HELD
DECEMBER 2, 2014

U.S. GOVERNMENT PUBLISHING OFFICE

91–816   WASHINGTON : 2015

For sale by the Superintendent of Documents, U.S. Government Publishing Office
Internet: bookstore.gpo.gov   Phone: toll free (866) 512–1800; DC area (202) 512–1800
Fax: (202) 512–2104   Mail: Stop IDCC, Washington, DC 20402–0001

CONTENTS

CHRONOLOGICAL LIST OF HEARINGS

2014

TUESDAY, DECEMBER 2, 2014

THE ROLE OF MARITIME AND AIR POWER IN DOD'S THIRD OFFSET STRATEGY

STATEMENTS PRESENTED BY MEMBERS OF CONGRESS

WITNESSES

APPENDIX

THE ROLE OF MARITIME AND AIR POWER IN DOD'S THIRD OFFSET STRATEGY

House of Representatives,
Committee on Armed Services,
Subcommittee on Seapower and Projection Forces,
Washington, DC, Tuesday, December 2, 2014.

The subcommittee met, pursuant to call, at 4:24 p.m., in room 2118, Rayburn House Office Building, Hon. J. Randy Forbes (chairman of the subcommittee) presiding.

OPENING STATEMENT OF HON. J. RANDY FORBES, A REPRESENTATIVE FROM VIRGINIA, CHAIRMAN, SUBCOMMITTEE ON SEAPOWER AND PROJECTION FORCES

Mr. FORBES. Gentlemen, thank you so much for your patience and putting up with us as we had these votes, and we are sorry to kind of flip you around.

We are kind of waiting for Mr. Langevin to get here. He is on his way. Mr. Courtney is ill and is not going to be with us. So if it is okay with you, I am going to go ahead and do the opening statement that we had planned to do. We weren't going to do that in the interest of time, but since we are waiting for Mr. Langevin, we will do that.

Today, the subcommittee convenes to receive testimony on the role of seapower and airpower in DOD's [Department of Defense] Defense Innovation Initiative offset strategy

Our panel of distinguished guests testifying before us are Mr. Robert Martinage, Senior Fellow, Center for Strategic and Budgetary Assessments; Mr. Shawn Brimley, Executive Vice President and Director of Studies for the Center for a New American Security; Mr. Andrew Hunter, Director, Defense-Industrial Initiatives Group, and Senior Fellow, International Security Program, Center for Strategic and International Studies; Mr. David Ochmanek, from the RAND Corporation.

And, gentlemen, we thank you for being with us today.

This past summer, Defense Secretary Chuck Hagel concluded in a speech at the Naval War College that we are entering an era where American dominance can no longer be taken for granted. This is a stunning admission that deserves the full and undivided attention of the Congress.

Today, states like China, Russia, Iran, and North Korea are investing in precision-guided munitions, advanced sensors, undersea warfare, unmanned systems, and offensive cyber and space capabilities to alter the military balance with the United States.

Nowhere are these risks more evident than in the Indo-Pacific region and specifically Northeast Asia, where the People's Republic

(1)

2

of China is using its growing economic and military power to coerce its neighbors and challenge the current American-led order.

China's investments in what it calls a "counterintervention strategy" are calling into question our ability to project power, degrading escalation dominance, forcing allies to doubt the credibility of our deterrent, and imposing costs on current joint force capabilities that will make it increasingly difficult to sustain the military edge.

In recent years, we witnessed various responses to these emerging challenges, including the establishment of the Air-Sea Battle Office, new weapons programs like the Long Range Anti-Ship Missile, and operational initiatives like the Air Force is pursuing in the Pacific. These efforts are all very much necessary, but they illustrate a larger concern: Alone and unguided by a true long-range strategic planning process, they are insufficient to prepare the Department of Defense for the future.

When Deputy Secretary of Defense Bob Work began discussing a new offset strategy this past summer, this subcommittee took notice. I read the available literature on the offset strategy of the late 1970s and the "New Look" of Eisenhower initiated in the 1950s and found in this history a useful analogy for today. Just like during these periods, we face new military operational dilemmas that cannot be resolved in our favor by doing more of the same.

I believe that the concept of peace through strength continues to be a sound maxim for guiding our defense policy, but, given the capabilities and new warfighting concepts our competitors are adopting, the answer cannot be just to build more military strength but to develop and invest in the right type of military strength.

We need to ask tough questions about the military competitions we find ourselves in, work to match our inherent military advantages and disadvantages against those of our competitors, and invest our time, energy, and resources in new ways to exploit our advantages and shift the military balance back in our favor.

I understand the Department of Defense has initiated the Defense Innovation Initiative to develop a new offset strategy to prepare the United States for emerging warfighting regimes. While I look forward to future testimony from the Pentagon about this effort, today's hearing provides an opportunity to enhance this subcommittee's understanding about the concept of an offset strategy and potential options the Pentagon can consider in pursuing this new initiative.

Finally, there is one important distinction that I believe needs to be made concerning the offset strategy from the 1970s. While there was a tremendous amount of intellectual capital and research and development dollars invested during this period to develop an offset for Soviet advantages, the resources to fund this effort never materialized. It was not until the Reagan military buildup in the early 1980s that the benefits of capabilities like stealth, precision-guided munitions, and sensors could be fielded in a way that actually exploited these new technologies and shifted the military balance in our favor.

Today, we face a similar dilemma. Absent a reversal of sequestration, we can develop brilliant ideas for a new offset strategy and still fall far short of our objective.

I again thank our panel for being here to testify and look forward to your testimony.

And, with that, we are still waiting for Mr. Langevin, but Ms. Hanabusa has joined us, and we are glad always to have her. And it looks like Mr. Kilmer is making his way down, and we certainly have Mr. Byrne with us. So we are going to go ahead and proceed with our testimony if that is okay.

With that, Mr. Martinage, I think you are first up. Is that my understanding?

[The prepared statement of Mr. Forbes can be found in the Appendix on page 29.]

STATEMENT OF ROBERT MARTINAGE, SENIOR FELLOW, CENTER FOR STRATEGIC AND BUDGETARY ASSESSMENTS

Mr. MARTINAGE. Chairman Forbes, members and staff of this distinguished subcommittee, thank you for the opportunity to share my views on the implications of a third offset strategy on air and maritime forces.

I would like to request that my full written statement be submitted for the record.

Mr. FORBES. Without objection, all of the written statements will be submitted for the record.

Mr. MARTINAGE. While several important lessons with contemporary relevance can be drawn from the New Look in the 1950s and the offset strategy adopted in the 1970s, I would like to focus my remarks this afternoon on the development of what Deputy Secretary of Defense Robert Work has dubbed a third offset strategy.

I would like to share my thoughts on four issues. First, why is an offset strategy needed? Or, put another way, what is the operational problem that we need to solve? Second, what enduring capability advantages might we leverage to enable a new operational approach to power projection? Third, what kind of shifts in the current DOD investment portfolio would be needed to enable this new concept of operations? And, finally, what isn't a third offset strategy?

So, to begin, we need a new offset strategy simply because traditional sources of U.S. military advantage are being eroded by the maturation and proliferation of disruptive technologies, most notably anti-access and area denial [A2/AD] capabilities, to state and nonstate actors alike.

While China's ongoing military modernization represents the pacing threat in the Asia-Pacific, prospective adversaries in other key regions around the globe are also acquiring and fielding a wide range of A2/AD capabilities to exploit U.S. vulnerabilities.

This trend is clear and disconcerting. Absent a major change in how the U.S. military projects power, its ability to deter aggression, reassure allies, and defend U.S. security interests will be increasingly challenged in the years ahead.

More specifically, the U.S. military faces four core operational problems that will become more severe over time. First, close-in regional bases—ports, airfields, ground installations—are increasingly vulnerable to attack in a growing number of countries around the world. Second, large surface combatants and aircraft carriers at sea are becoming easier to detect, track, and engage extended-range from an adversary's coast. Third, nonstealthy aircraft are becoming more vulnerable to being shot down by modern integrated air defense networks. And, space is no longer a sanctuary from attack.

Given the increasing scale and diversity of these threats, trying to counter them symmetrically with tailored forces or competing missile for missile is likely to be both futile and unaffordable over the long run. The United States cannot afford to simply scale up the current mix of joint power projection capabilities. Similarly, while active defenses and countermeasures may be tactically effective and operationally useful in some situations, they must not be allowed to crowd out offensive capability and capacity, which is the foundation upon which deterrence is built.

Turning now to my second point, to solve this growing problem, I believe we should take advantage of U.S. core competencies in unmanned systems and automation, extended-range and low-observable air operations, undersea warfare, and complex systems engineering and integration.

Importantly, when I say "core competency," I don't mean just technology. It is not just about gadgets but, rather, the combination of technology, our industrial base, skilled manpower, training, doctrine, and hard-to-learn practical experience that confers the capability advantage that is difficult for rivals to duplicate or counter.

As part of a new offset strategy, these enduring U.S. capability advantages could enable U.S. power projection across the threat spectrum to deter aggression, reassure our friends and allies, and defend our national security interests.

More specifically, they could provide the basis for a global surveillance and strike network that would be balanced, in that it would comprise a mix of low-end and high-end platforms aligned to a widely varying threat environment; resilient, in that it would be geographically distributed with less dependence upon close-in bases, have greatly reduced sensitivity to enemy air defense capabilities, and be significantly more tolerant of disruptions to space-based systems.

It would be responsive, in that a credible surveillance strike presence could be generated quickly by taking advantage of rapid global reach and survivable forward presence. And, lastly, it would be scalable, in that the network could be expanded to influence events in multiple locations around the world concurrently.

While many elements of the U.S. military would have important roles to play in a future global surveillance and strike network, it would emphasize air and maritime forces. In particular, it would leverage increasingly autonomous unmanned systems, given their advantages in terms of ultra-long mission endurance and low life-cycle costs relative to manned platforms.

So now to my third topic: What shifts in the defense investment portfolio would we need to realize this type of new operational concept?

I address this question in considerably more detail in my written statement, but, in short, I think the portfolio needs to be rebalanced in three ways: increase space resiliency and fielding hedges against degradation of space-based capabilities; expanding undersea payload capacity and flexibility; and, third, increasing the combat radius and survivability of land- and sea-based airpower.

Simply put, it is imperative to rectify the growing imbalance between forces that are able to operate only in permissive environments versus those that can operate in non-permissive environments as well.

So now to my fourth and final topic, which is: What isn't the third offset strategy, in my view? Three quick points.

First, it is not a comprehensive national defense strategy, let alone a national security strategy. It does not address every threat facing the Nation, but, rather, should focus more narrowly on restoring and sustaining our conventional power projection capability and capacity, which is a sine qua non of a superpower and the bedrock of deterrence.

Second, it is not about offsetting sequestration or the Budget Control Act. Don't get me wrong; I strongly support rescinding the Budget Control Act, eliminating sequestration, and funding defense at a higher level. That said, the changes in the defense investment portfolio that I outlined earlier are needed irrespective of the budget level.

Third, it is not just about technology. It is about identifying the operational problems that we face, leveraging our enduring capability advantages to address them, and technology is just but one component of that.

Lastly, I would just like to conclude by saying that we just cannot afford to continue the current business-as-usual approach to power projection nor plan on having the resources and time to rectify the many problems with the current path once they become fully manifest. So it is really essential for Congress, and this committee in particular, to take an active role in driving the formulation and implementation of a third offset strategy.

I look forward to your questions and discussion. Thank you.

[The prepared statement of Mr. Martinage can be found in the Appendix on page 32.]

Mr. FORBES. Thank you, Mr. Martinage.

Mr. Brimley.

STATEMENT OF SHAWN BRIMLEY, EXECUTIVE VICE PRESIDENT AND DIRECTOR OF STUDIES, CENTER FOR A NEW AMERICAN SECURITY

Mr. BRIMLEY. Thank you, Chairman Forbes, members and staff, for the opportunity to testify. I want to acknowledge my co-panelists, whose work I very much admire.

I want to thank this committee for delving into the issue of how the Pentagon's new Defense Innovation Initiative can be fully harnessed for the long-term military technical competition unfolding today.

It is a contest over military technical superiority and whether the U.S. can sustain its advantage deep into the 21st century or be overtaken by its competitors. This strategic competition will be played out over decades, and it is one the U.S. could very well lose.

America's Armed Forces must project and sustain power across oceans and be able to perform complex offensive and defensive operations in all types of geographic terrain and in all operating domains. No other nation-state requires this kind of global power projection capability to adequately protect its national interests. The U.S. is unique in this regard.

But after over 25 years of U.S. power projection being the source of our unique advantage, today it forms the basis for a long-term military competition.

To properly frame the so-called third offset strategy, it is necessary to place it in context. In my written statement, I describe how military history can be divided into two basic eras or regimes: the unguided-weapons regime and the guided-weapons regime.

The key characteristic of the unguided-weapons regime was that most munitions that were thrown, shot, fired, launched, or dropped ultimately missed their targets. Therefore, in order to maximize success at the point of attack, commanders would need to aggregate their forces to achieve a—often achieve numerical superiority.

The crucible of World War II and the early Cold War period drove the development of two alternative ways for the U.S. to compensate or offset the numerical advantages our adversaries often enjoyed.

The first offset strategy centered on atomic weapons. The massive destructive—the destructive power inherent in a nuclear blast obviated the need for much accuracy. This was initially attractive to the United States as a means to compensate for insufficient land forces in Europe, but as the Soviet Union approached basic parity in the nuclear balance, the advantage that the U.S. enjoyed faded quickly. This perceived erosion in U.S. deterrence drove the search for a new way to offset Soviet conventional military power.

The second offset strategy that reduced the need for mass on the battlefield came in the form of guided conventional weapons that actively corrected their trajectories after being fired, released, or launched. Transformative technologies like stealth, the Global Positioning System, and the broader revolution in computer networking acted as a critical means to employ guided munitions against an adversary. Put simply, guided weapons ushered in an entirely new warfighting regime, one in which accuracy became independent of range.

Because the U.S. moved first and moved decisively into the guided-munitions era, our Armed Forces gained a competitive advantage that helped to reinforce our conventional deterrent and was an influential variable, I think, in how the Cold War ended.

For a quarter-century, the United States has continued to benefit from its initial first-mover advantages in guided munitions. But as both Secretary Hagel and Deputy Secretary Work, among others, have recently described, we are fast approaching a world in which the guided-munitions regime is fully mature, with a much broader range of players now fully invested. U.S. defense planners must now assume that future adversaries will employ sophisticated battle networks and advanced guided munitions to oppose U.S. military forces.

We see this dynamic being played out most clearly in Asia, where China is moving quickly into the guided-weapons era with a goal to establishing a degree of guided-weapons parity in an extensive maritime contested zone.

So I believe the essential strategic challenge the Pentagon faces is how to ensure that our Armed Forces can deter and defeat an adversary that has established a degree of guided-weapons parity. We have never encountered this kind of strategic environment before, and I believe this has to be the primary focus of the Pentagon's strategic planning and force development efforts.

So the third offset strategy will need to explore many issues. For instance, in my mind, the Pentagon needs to determine how best to, one, defend against long-range guided munitions at more favorable cost exchange ratios; two, ensure U.S. aircraft carriers can project and sustain striking power beyond adversary missile ranges, and I think this committee has done great work in this regard; three, establish greater magazine capacity to ensure our forces can engage in multiple rounds of a salvable competition with an adversary employing guided munitions; and, four, maintain resilience in our own guided-munitions battle networks as plausible adversaries develop ways to contest and degrade our command and control links.

I would encourage Members to review my colleague Bob Martinage's recent report on this topic, where he lays out a series of strategy and spending priorities that I believe constitute an excellent guide for the budget cycles ahead.

But as you adjudicate, scrutinize, and shape DOD's strategy and spending priorities in the years ahead, I would encourage you to hold the Pentagon accountable for the priorities articulated by its leadership and also hope that you assist them in providing the top cover necessary for implementing the choices in the years ahead.

DOD, as you know, is a massive bureaucracy that tends to resist even needed course corrections. But I think a window of opportunity now exists where the strategic environment and the fiscal pressure require real choices, and the leadership here on Capitol Hill and at the Pentagon can firmly move the Department such that America's military technical advantage can be sustained in the decades ahead.

Thank you again for having me.

[The prepared statement of Mr. Brimley can be found in the Appendix on page 44.]

Mr. FORBES. Thank you, Mr. Brimley.

Mr. Hunter.

STATEMENT OF ANDREW HUNTER, DIRECTOR, DEFENSE–IN-DUSTRIAL INITIATIVES GROUP, AND SENIOR FELLOW, INTERNATIONAL SECURITY PROGRAM, CENTER FOR STRA-TEGIC AND INTERNATIONAL STUDIES

Mr. HUNTER. Chairman Forbes, Mr. Langevin, thank you very much for the opportunity to testify today on the Department of Defense offset strategy and its implication for the role of maritime and air power.

It is an honor to appear as a witness before this committee, my former professional home, and a place where the critical national security questions of our time have been and I believe always will be thoroughly reviewed.

And I can't help but take notice of Chairman Skelton's portrait. It was an honor to serve him on the staff, and a pleasure to see so many of his colleagues with whom he served and for whom he cared so deeply.

The topic of today's hearing is an important one. The Department of Defense's recently announced Defense Innovation Initiative, which is tasked to develop and support a new offset strategy, is a serious effort to achieve an important strategic objective. And that objective is to leverage innovation, both operational and technological, to extend the Department's advantage over potential adversaries even if those adversaries engage in carefully planned aggressive and increasingly successful efforts to erode that advantage.

The Defense Innovation Initiative must establish a concrete plan to achieve this objective, and Congress must ensure that the Department is resourced and organized to pursue that plan.

Now let me propose a few ways for the committee to assess the offset strategy as it is being developed.

It is critical that the use of innovation as an offset strategy is integrated within a broader national strategy. Only in a broad strategic context can it be determined which capabilities, and therefore which innovative concepts and technologies, merit enhanced investment. The 2012 Defense Strategic Guidance, the QDR [Quadrennial Defense Review], ultimately the National Security Strategy must provide this strategic context.

If you read these strategic documents today, they specify a remarkably wide range of missions U.S. forces will need to be able to perform in the future, and they cite the need for new capabilities in the critical domains of cyber and space. Now, to address a mission set this diverse, the next offset strategy will have to focus on capabilities with a broad array of applications, from the high end to the low end of conflict.

I believe there is a real danger of over-specifying the problem, particularly if you are specifying it at one end of the spectrum solely. As such, it is my view that the next offset strategy should consist of a set of targeted capabilities that enable new operational concepts and be paired with a technology investment roadmap.

I don't believe the next investment strategy—offset strategy should be a list of platform-specific investments. Now, that necessary step comes later and, I think, should come through a separate process, through the budget process.

To be effective, the next offset strategy needs to guide action by industry as well as by the Department of Defense so that the Department's investments are fully leveraged. Communication with industry, therefore, including to the maximum extent possible with nontraditional suppliers, is a key enabler that will—as will the ability to harvest commercial technologies. And the strategy must be flexible enough to adjust for unforeseen adversary capabilities.

And, lastly, I want to point out that there are inevitably tradeoffs between developing new capabilities and operational concepts and then maintaining existing ones. We must, however, be careful not to throw out the baby with the bathwater as we shift our investment strategy.

Now, I believe future adversaries are likely to pursue cost-imposing strategies that seek to raise the economic and military stakes for U.S. military actions to levels that they believe will be unacceptable to the American public. The U.S. must pursue capabilities that enable effective responses at acceptable costs.

I do not claim to be able to lay out a fully developed offset strategy for you today that meets all of the requirements I have described so far. Developing such an approach will take time and much discussion with relevant stakeholders, and I think war-gaming and experimentations to test out these ideas will be critical.

However, it is my expectation that the next offset strategy will extend many of the capabilities developed as part of the last offset strategy, as they are likely to be highly relevant when addressing future challenges.

Most notably, I believe battlespace awareness capabilities will be critical, if not the critical element of future conflicts, both high-end and low-end. Given the rapid pace of development in areas such as data mining, sensor fusion, image and video processing, significant advances in battlespace awareness are likely to become available in coming years. And such advances can significantly enhance the ability of U.S. forces to plan and execute successful missions at acceptable cost.

Denying battlespace awareness to adversaries may present even greater opportunities. The ability of U.S. forces to act cooperatively with partner forces can provide access to additional sensors and information that enhance our awareness while significantly complicating potential adversaries' ability to impose costs on the United States.

These capabilities readily lend themselves to the air and maritime realm. AWACS [Airborne Warning and Control System], Combined Engagement Capability, are networked approaches that were pioneered by the Air Force and Navy and provide exactly the kind of the battlespace awareness that is likely to be key in future conflicts. The Marine Corps Distributed Operations concept applied a similar conceptual approach to control of terrain in Iraq and Afghanistan. And the Army and JIEDDO [Joint Improvised Explosive Device Defeat Organization] developed integrated sensor networks for the protection of U.S. forward operating bases that achieved significant enhancements in capability. These approaches can be extended and applied to other mission areas.

The support for the funding and flexibility needed for the Department to adopt innovative approaches is far and away the most important role Congress can play in the development of the next offset strategy. In an era of declining budgets, it is all too easy to decrement investments in innovation in order to pay readiness bills or to pay bills resulting from the failure to make needed changes in force structure or compensation.

The risk to innovation is by no means theoretical. CSIS [Center for Strategic and International Studies] research shows that contract spending for research and development dropped by 21 percent in fiscal year 2013, the first year of sequestration, significantly more than the overall 10 percent drop in the defense budget under sequestration and more than the 16 percent drop in all contract spending. It will require the active support of Congress to ensure that innovation is enabled and not stifled by these dynamics.

A significant opportunity for Congress to facilitate the next offset strategy comes from reducing barriers to the adoption of innovation approaches. Such approaches require relatively open communication with industry and careful tailoring of the acquisition process. For systems under design, modular open systems approaches can be utilized to enable the rapid incorporation of innovative capabilities throughout system lifecycles.

Most critically, Congress can support easier access to commercial technologies. Existing statutory requirements, such as the Truth in Negotiations Act [TINA] and the Cost Accounting Standards [CAS], were designed to protect the government's interest in acquiring technology from firms that engage in both government and non-government work. While these statutes address real issues in the government-industry relationship, the implementation mechanisms for these systems are not well aligned with modern commercial practices. A careful review of TINA and CAS could substantially enhance the Department of Defense's ability to access cutting-edge technology.

In closing, I commend the committee's decision to focus on DOD's next offset strategy at this hearing and recommend the committee continue to follow this effort closely. Congressional support for change is likely to prove decisive to success.

[The prepared statement of Mr. Hunter can be found in the Appendix on page 54.]

Mr. FORBES. Mr. Hunter, we are glad to have you back before the committee, and I know Chairman Skelton would be very proud of where you have gone in your career.

Mr. Ochmanek.

STATEMENT OF DAVID OCHMANEK, RAND CORPORATION

Mr. OCHMANEK. Thank you, Chairman Forbes, Mr. Langevin, other members and staff of the committee. And thank you for the opportunity to testify before you today.

You have posed a difficult and important question here. We know that maritime and air forces will play crucial roles in any future conflict against the most capable adversaries we face, but we don't know precisely what roles those forces will play. And that is because the nature of the challenge posed by the most capable adversaries we face, particularly those wielding sophisticated A2/AD [anti-access/area denial] capabilities, is so extensive that the United States, at this point, has to rethink its entire approach to power projection. And, therefore, it will be premature to make conclusions about what roles particular force elements will play.

Members of this committee are all familiar with the types of threats that cause us the most concern. I won't rehash them here. And, as Congressman Forbes and my colleagues have observed, China is the leading exponent of these types of threats but not the only one.

Since the end of the Cold War, we have come, rightly, to expect that when U.S. forces are committed to combat against the conventional forces of a state adversary they will win quick and lopsided victories. Looking to the future, when we think about combat against the most capable plausible adversaries, we will have to revise these expectations.

In such conflicts, should they occur, U.S. forces will have to fight, and fight hard, for the sorts of advantages that we have come to take nearly for granted in conflicts over the past few years—air superiority, maritime superiority, space superiority, and the ability to operate forces forward largely from sanctuary. We can't take those for granted anymore.

Put most starkly, the legacy concepts of operation that our forces have used so successfully in recent years will not work against the forces of the most capable adversaries in the future or, at a minimum, won't produce satisfactory results.

The third offset strategy, which seeks to focus and energize technology, development, and systems engineering, is intended to rectify this problem, and, in response, one can only say, "Bravo." But this effort, while necessary, will not in and of itself be sufficient. It will need to be supported and complemented by several related activities, and I will mention five here.

One, DOD needs to revive and reconstitute its capacity for joint operational analysis and gaming. The joint community's ability to conduct quantitative assessments of the capabilities of future forces has atrophied in recent years, and this capability is essential for all force planning. We especially need more iterative, rigorously adjudicated, tabletop war games to allow operators to test their nascent ideas about potential new operational concepts against an intelligent reactive red team.

Two, new approaches are required for basing and operating our forces in contested theaters. Too often in the war-gaming we have done, when the blue team tries to strengthen deterrence during a simulated crisis by reinforcing the theater, it ends up actually projecting vulnerability rather than projecting power, creating lucrative targets for the enemy's long-range precision strike assets. We need more survivable ways to base and operate our forces in these theaters.

Three, we should do more to help our partners and allies field more capable self-defense forces. We should not try to solve this challenge on our own. Allies and partners can impose smaller-scale A2/AD challenges of their own to states that threaten them. And enhancements like this can't take the place of U.S. forces and commitment, but analysis suggests there is a lot of unexploited potential there.

Four, not to be crass, DOD will need more money. It is very difficult to see how even a flawlessly executed third offset approach could be sufficient to meet growing challenges if the limits imposed by the Budget Control Act are not lifted in fiscal year 2016 and beyond.

And, finally, number five, as Secretary Hagel has observed, Congress has to be a full partner in this. If DOD is going to spend more money on new and urgently needed capabilities, it will have to spend less on lower-priority programs. This will call for things like continued adjustments to force structure and end strength, garnering savings in pay and benefits, eliminating unneeded base infrastructure—all hard to do, easy to say, I know, but very important if we are going to actually get the level of effort against this new effort that is called for.

In conclusion, I would say that the most credible deterrent to aggression is one that confronts the adversary with the prospect of failure at the operational level. Without question, mounting a robust defense of this nature is becoming more challenging for the United States, and, indeed, some people in this country are already saying it is too hard, it is too costly, we can't do it.

But future U.S. forces, I believe, properly modernized, properly postured, and employed with the forces of regional allies and partners, should be capable of posing very serious obstacles to aggression by even our most sophisticated adversaries. This, as I understand it, is the central goal of the new offset strategy. I believe it is a worthy and achievable objective.

Thank you, and I look forward to your questions.

[The prepared statement of Mr. Ochmanek can be found in the Appendix on page 68.]

Mr. FORBES. Gentlemen, thank you all for your statements, and thanks for your written statements.

I am going to defer my questions until the end. And since Mr. Byrne was the first one at the hearing today, we are going to recognize him first for 5 minutes for any questions he may have.

Mr. BYRNE. Gentlemen, we appreciate you being here today.

One of the things, as a new member of the committee, that strikes me about the position we find ourselves in is that decisions that were made before I got here—and I am not trying to second-guess them—have put us in a posture where we don't necessarily have the capacity to catch up as quickly as we would like.

Is there one thing that you would focus on, one precise thing that you could tell this committee that we should focus on that could get us back into the game at a level that we need to be in?

Those are easy questions, I know.

Mr. BRIMLEY. Maybe I will take the first stab at that, sir.

I mean, I would look to the recent hearings that this committee has held. A good example, in my mind, is making sure that the carrier air wing can fully project and sustain strike power in these kinds of contested environments. And so making sure that, however the Navy or however the DOD finalizes the requirements on the UCLASS, the Unmanned Carrier-Launched Airborne Surveillance and Strike vehicle, whether it is for a lightly contested environment or for a more high-end environment, to me, that is one of the canary—a canary in the coal mine.

You know, if DOD is really serious about fully exploiting the advantages inherent in a long-range, unmanned strike platform, that requirements debate is something I am paying a lot of attention to because that, I think—how that goes in the next 3 or 4 months I think will indicate how serious the Department is in fully moving into this more unmanned autonomous warfighting regime.

We have got to find a way for the aircraft carrier to remain very relevant at range when faced with one of these high-end, anti-access/area denial challenges. If we fail to do that, it is hard for me to understand how we can project and sustain power with our allies and partners and maintain the conventional deterrence that we need to provide security in the Asia-Pacific as one example.

Mr. HUNTER. From my perspective—I recently departed the Department of Defense—the capability that I perceive to be the single most limited—the highest-demand, most limited capacity that the Department has is intelligence, surveillance, and reconnaissance. When a new mission comes on board, that is the thing that the

COCOM [combatant commander] is most interested and gets the least of that they are looking for at the start of a conflict.

So I would say that is a good place to look. And, frankly, that really informed my thinking about the criticality of battlespace awareness in future conflicts.

Mr. OCHMANEK. I would broaden it a little bit, Congressman. If we think about recent applications of U.S. military power, when the President presses the ''go'' button, we expect that with hours, if not days, U.S. forces will dominate all five domains of warfare—air, land, sea, space, and cyberspace. We have to disabuse ourselves of that notion in the future.

So we have to find ways to reach in to the contested airspace, maritime space, and not only detect but also strike the enemy's operational centers of gravity, whether it is naval ships, amphibious ships making an invasion, aircraft, combat aircraft. And I think standoff weapons are a way to do that. ISR [intelligence, surveillance, and reconnaissance] systems that can survive in highly contested air defense environments are ways to do that.

But that is sort of the single operational problem I would focus on as a priority.

Mr. MARTINAGE. To build on that, I would take it up maybe even one step higher and just say, when you look at the air and maritime investment portfolio, it is heavily weighted towards capabilities that operate in low- to medium-threat environments or permissive environments. We need to shift the balance and have relatively more capabilities that can project power in non-permissive environments, the higher-end threat environments.

I know you asked for one, but I am going to have to throw one more in. And that is we need to do something to streamline the acquisition process. It takes too long to field new capabilities, and, you know, in many cases, they are almost obsolete by the time they field. And we just need to get faster and more agile in terms of our exploitation of R&D [research and development].

Mr. BYRNE. Thank you, Mr. Chairman.

Mr. FORBES. The chair recognizes Ms. Hanabusa, who we are going to miss very much from this committee, and we have enjoyed having her and her service to our country.

Ms. HANABUSA. Thank you. Thank you, Mr. Chair.

As many of you may be aware, the chairman and I had this wonderful series of hearings basically on what does it mean to pivot to Asia-Pacific. And, as you can imagine, as someone who represents Hawaii, when we talk about the pivot to Asia-Pacific, I have gone on and say, well, it is an air and sea issue. If you know anything about how large the Pacific Ocean is, it is air and sea. Of course, it doesn't play well with, in particular, Army, because they don't like the fact that we are saying it is an air and sea situation.

So isn't one of the most critical aspects that we have to deal with is really, I guess, the territoriality or the protection of the various branches and the fact that we have funded in the past with everyone sort of sharing equally and if we are pivoting to Asia-Pacific, for example, it cannot really continue with a, quote, ''equal share''?

So, as we look at what is this offset strategy, don't we have to first begin by looking at the structure of the DOD, how the DOD apportions its resources? And if it continues with a basic assumption that everyone will share, then how do we then shift to the point where we are looking at, for example, carrier strength, submarine strength?

You know, a very good friend of mine and mentor, Senator Inouye, always said to me, "You know, we used to rule the seven seas after World War II. We don't do that anymore, but we will always rule, or we should always rule, the deep blue sea."

So, in that scenario, if you would all look at it in terms of the offset strategy, I can't get past the major assumptions that I think DOD makes. Even with the QDR that we just went over, DOD makes certain kinds of assumptions that I don't think necessarily fits in your strategy.

Is there any one of you who wants to tackle that? And if you want to tell me I am wrong, that is fine too. But, you know, I think when we talk about the pivot, we've got issues, and it is in line with what you are looking at for the offset strategy.

Mr. OCHMANEK. Congresswoman, if I might make a suggestion or throw out an idea, I agree with you that when we come through the process of designing a concept of operations and a force that will be appropriate for this new demanding environment, things will look different. We will have different apportionment of roles and missions across the services, different budget shares, and so forth.

But I think form follows function. And my lead-off remarks suggested that we don't know today exactly how we would fight this fight in 2020 and 2025. I think that as we figure that out, through analysis, experimentation, field exercises and tests, we will get insights about the capabilities that we need. And the forces, if we are successful in planning and fielding the appropriate force, will come along to fulfill that concept.

Ms. HANABUSA. I agree with you. But let me add this, though. You know, if we can't know what we are going to do in 2020 or 2025, we in Congress are making those policy calls, and I—after one of the CSIS hearings, as a matter of fact, I said, I know how we do things now. We set policy by acquisition. As we acquire, we are setting policy.

And that is—2020 is right around the corner. And as we go through the NDAA [National Defense Authorization Act] and as we go through the appropriation measures, we are setting the policies that are going to affect 2020. So one of the most frustrating parts about sitting on this side has been you want us to wait and see what it is going to do, but we have to appropriate and set the authorization early on.

So how do we come and do that and then incorporate this offset strategy, which I agree with? I just don't know how it all melds together.

Mr. MARTINAGE. I think you raise an excellent point. I mean, really, right now, we are building the Air Force and the Navy of 2030 and 2040 and beyond. So I think that it is an excellent point.

I mean, in terms of the offset strategy in dealing with the challenges in the Pacific, I think, generally, basing resiliency and dispersion is a big issue, as well as longer-range, more survivable aircraft—both manned and unmanned—and undersea, exploiting the undersea, as you said, both submarines and UUVs [unmanned underwater vehicles] and other payloads.

How all that sorts out in terms of budget share, I guess we will need to see. But the point I would stress, though, is that, whether it is the offset strategy or the pivot to the Pacific, those aren't comprehensive national defense strategies. We still have other challenges around the world—you know, subconventional aggression in Europe, you know, in the Ukraine, counterinsurgencies in various places in the world, counterterrorism. Those are all places where, you know, ground forces, the Army and the Marine Corps, have important roles to play.

So we have to just figure out what the right capability and capacity balance is across these various types of contingencies.

I am not sure if that exactly answered it.

Ms. HANABUSA. Thank you.

And I yield back.

Mr. FORBES. Mr. Coffman is recognized for 5 minutes.

Mr. COFFMAN. Thank you, Mr. Chairman.

A couple questions. The first one is, in terms of the projection of seapower, the carrier has been central to that. And if you look at the Chinese, they realize they are never going to match us carrier for carrier, so they are focused on some, I guess you might call it an asymmetric measure or the anti-ship ballistic missile.

How—I mean, is it still important for us to put so many of our eggs in that one basket as a platform for the projection of seapower?

Anybody who wants——

Mr. BRIMLEY. Maybe I will just quickly.

To build on what Mr. Martinage was talking about, you know, the aircraft—and knows better than I do, certainly—the carriers we are fielding today are going to be with us for 40-plus years. And so, for me, as sort of a policy analyst, you know, and to put a pun on it, you know, that ship has sailed. So the question for me is, how do we make sure that that investment, that sunk cost——

Mr. COFFMAN. Well, I mean, 11—do we maintain in the future——

Mr. BRIMLEY. That is right.

Mr. COFFMAN [continuing]. 11 carriers?

Mr. BRIMLEY. That is right.

So the question for me is, how do we make sure that what flies off of that carrier can make that investment sound when we look at the operational challenges we will face 5, 10, 15 years from now?

That is why, for me, in terms of this question, it is the carrier air wing that is the key. And if you can fully push the Navy—in my mind, if you can fully push the Navy to embrace what I see as the inherent benefits of moving decisively into the unmanned, more autonomous regime where you can really get some cost-benefit analysis and get an unmanned system to be able to penetrate and strike at distance and at range, that makes the aircraft carrier highly relevant even 20, 25, 30 years out.

A separate question is, you know, what is the long-term future of the capital ship? Some analysts have suggested that over time the A2/AD environment may get so bad that the competition tends to go under the surface. And you see indications of that now. You see senior leaders spending a lot of rhetorical time and effort talking about making sure we maintain our submarine advantages. I think that is the critical, sort of, corollary to your question, sir.

Mr. HUNTER. I would just say on that, I agree with the point about the sunk costs. We have these carriers. They provide incredible capability. We don't want to lose that. They are being threatened. And there are things that we should do in terms of having capabilities with increased range and with low observability. But that does take you down the path where the cost-imposing strategy is working. In other words, you are playing into the cost-imposing strategy, because long-range and very low-observable platforms tend to be fairly expensive.

What we relied on in the past to protect the carrier was the fact that it was hard to find. And it is becoming increasingly easier to find because adversaries are using more networked approaches, as we did long ago.

We simply didn't focus, I believe, on how to defeat those capabilities, their battlespace awareness, their ability to find us, because it is so new that these capabilities belong to anyone except us. And I think the most cost-effective way I can think of to go after that is to go directly after their ability to find and detect our assets.

Mr. COFFMAN. The last question is: Speaking to airpower and the future of the manned bomber that the Air Force wants versus unmanned or existing platforms—and I think that the argument for the next generation of manned bomber is, well, what if, i.e., communications were cut off, you would still be able to execute a mission, versus an unmanned platform.

I mean, in terms of the investment and the alternative uses of those dollars, is that a viable argument?

Mr. OCHMANEK. We did some work on that some years ago, Congressman. The marginal cost of actually putting human beings inside that platform is fairly low.

Mr. COFFMAN. Okay.

Mr. OCHMANEK. And when Secretary Gates approved the program, he specified that it should be optionally manned so that we have the choice, as we field these things, to send them out with crews or without crews.

Mr. COFFMAN. Okay.

Mr. OCHMANEK. So we will have flexibility as we build the overall platform to employ it in different ways.

And you are right; how confident we are about the resiliency of that communication link will be a key factor in whether or not it will be viable as an unmanned platform.

Mr. COFFMAN. Okay.

Mr. OCHMANEK. So I think we have covered—covered down on that.

Mr. COFFMAN. Okay. Great.

Thank you, Mr. Chairman. I yield back.

Mr. FORBES. Mr. Langevin is recognized for 5 minutes.

Mr. LANGEVIN. Thank you, Mr. Chairman.

I want to welcome our panel here today. Thank you for your testimony.

And, Mr. Hunter, in particular, welcome back before the committee. It is great to see you again.

So I appreciate the discussion that we are having and the comments you have made.

And, Mr. Brimley, in particular, I appreciate the comments you made on UCLASS. We talk about developing the standoff technologies. I think these types of things are going to be essential.

And in terms of what we should be doing, actually, one only has to look at what our adversaries are doing and what would hold our assets and our capabilities at risk. And, certainly, developing platforms that are most robust, that are standoff, that allow for deep penetration are the things that we need to focus on more heavily.

So I am watching very closely the Pentagon's decision as they design the requirements on UCLASS to see where that is going to come down. I think that will be very telling about how they are thinking and if they are getting this right.

But, obviously, innovation is going to be key to all of this and developing these new capabilities. And no matter which way the innovation tree branches, there are a few constraints that will be limiting factors.

But if I could, just for a minute, to focus particularly on the undersea, the *Virginia*-class program of record is well known, and the trend, of course, for the number of platforms and the payload space that they will have, particularly as the SSGNs [cruise missile submarines] age out and VPM [*Virginia* Payload Module] slowly builds into the fleet. The picture in terms of the numbers that we need isn't necessarily a pretty one, particularly when we look at programs like the LDUUV [Large Displacement Unmanned Undersea Vehicle], whose threshold requirements for the integration with VPM and *Virginia*-class boats with dry-dock shelters.

So are we investing in enough payload capacity to enable these future mission and technology constructs?

And, Mr. Martinage, maybe we would start with you and go down the line.

Mr. MARTINAGE. In my view, increasing undersea payload capacity and flexibility is a critical thing that we need to look at as part of the offset strategy. I think we gain a lot of advantage from our undersea warfare capabilities. And, as you alluded to, on the current trajectory, our undersea payload capacity is going to shrink by over 60 percent when the SSGNs retire in 2028 and the declining LA [*Los Angeles*] class are retired more quickly than they are being replaced by *Virginia*.

So, at the time we want to be increasing undersea capacity, it is actually going down rather dramatically. So the question is, how do we deal with that?

One is I think, absolutely, we have to get on board with *Virginia* Payload Module. It looks like we are heading in the right direction, but, again, that needs to be fully funded.

Then, looking at other options, undersea payload modules is a program that DARPA [Defense Advanced Research Projects Agency] is looking at, which would be payloads that are external to the submarine that could be deployed in peacetime or in period of crisis, but it would be a means to increase payload capacity but outside the submarine.

And then, lastly, taking advantage of UUVs, like the large-diameter UUV, and a family of UUVs, I think, is really critical. I think that is another high-payoff area with unmanned systems and automation that could help us increase the geographic coverage of our limited submarine fleet by having the unmanned systems extend their reach and their flexibility.

The other thing is that I think we want to look at new types of payloads for our submarines. Right now, it is fundamentally torpedoes and Tomahawks. It doesn't have to be that way. There is a variety of new weapons that they could take on, in terms of electronic attack or decoys or going after enemy air defenses, going after aircraft. There is a wide range of other things submarines could do that we should actively explore.

Mr. LANGEVIN. But do we have a right balance in terms of investing enough in payload capacity and enabling these future missions? What do you think?

Mr. MARTINAGE. My personal view is we need to shift the overall composition of the fleet over time increasingly to undersea and shift some of the resources that currently is going into the surface combatant force structure and modernization, shifting that balance—however much we need to determine—more towards the undersea for the reasons that we have talked about.

Mr. LANGEVIN. Thank you.

Anyone else want to comment?

Mr. OCHMANEK. I think, looking forward, undersea launch platforms and standoff attack means are good bets for this contested environment. And VPM is the option immediately available to us.

Mr. LANGEVIN. So could I ask this? Are the current organizational structures within the services robust enough, independent enough, and agile enough to drive innovative tactics, procedures, and technologies and the like into the operational forces? And how does today's status compare to the structure that produced the innovative ideas of past offset strategies?

Mr. HUNTER. I think this builds a little bit on Ms. Hanabusa's question, as well, because the question is, you know, can the services accept innovation? Because it does threaten existing capabilities, existing infrastructure for which there are strong advocates within the Department.

And one of the reasons why I recommended that the strategy be focused more on capabilities than on platforms is because I think, when you get into platforms, it is inevitably, well, I have my platform and you have your platform and now we are going to fight each other over who wins.

I think at the level of capability, it is not necessarily—as in some cases there are clear service, you know, areas of excellence. But at the level of capability, all of the services have an opportunity to at least make a case for how they can provide that capability, what can they bring to the table. So I think it changes the conversation a little bit less to one about rice bowls and more about what folks can actually do and bring to the table.

Mr. LANGEVIN. Thank you.

Mr. MARTINAGE. On that point, I would just reiterate a point that Dave Ochmanek made during his presentation about the need for joint operational analysis and war-gaming. I think that is one of the tools that could help build confidence that these are new operational concepts that we need to exploit and these are the types of enabling technologies we need for those concepts to work. And I think that is just an important tool for building that confidence and driving that change.

Mr. LANGEVIN. Very good. I share that. Thank you.

I yield back, Mr. Chairman.

Mr. FORBES. As you guys know, Mr. Langevin has been a leader in these issues on this committee and the full committee, and we appreciate his leadership in all of that.

I want to wrap up now by telling you two things. First of all, this has been a very important hearing for us, and it is just the beginning. And we are probably going to follow up with some written questions, if that is okay with you, to get on the record.

Mr. Byrne and I were in a meeting earlier today when we heard the majority leader give us a cute little analogy, but he talked about four frogs sitting on a log—or maybe he said five. I forgot what it was. But let's say it was five frogs sitting on a log, and four of them decided to jump off. How many was left? And the answer was five, because there is a big difference between deciding and doing. And so we want to make sure that we go from just talking about this to doing it.

And assuming we do that, we—Mr. Brimley, you have been very clear that this shouldn't be a defense strategy. I think everybody is pretty much agreeing with that, that we should narrow the focus of this down.

So I am going ask you four questions. You can pick any one of them you want, or all of them, and use it as, kind of, each of your closing remarks.

But first thing, all of our strategies and our budgets are built on assumptions. If you had to pick two of the assumptions that we are using today that you think are wrong or either could very probably be wrong, what would those two assumptions be?

The second thing is: How do we do what Mr. Brimley has suggested we do and focus our efforts? In other words, if we weren't going to shotgun this and bring it into a focus, the next two steps that we take from here, what would you recommend that those two steps be?

And then the third one is: This a partnership, but more and more this is no longer just a partnership between DOD and Congress; it is also the private sector. And we are depending more and more upon their creativity and what they bring to the table. How do we get them involved in this process but yet try to protect our intellectual property rights so that we are not having all this stolen around the globe?

And then the fourth part of that, each of you have mentioned the importance of our allies. How do we do more to encourage our allies to be a part of this strength thing?

And, Mr. Ochmanek, why don't we start with you, and we will just work backwards down the line and finish up.

Mr. OCHMANEK. Thank you, Mr. Chairman. I will take a swing at two of those pitches.

First, with regard to the next two steps, not to be a broken record on this, but I think careful analysis of the problem can help us focus from the outset on what we think the most important operational challenges are.

As we discussed before we came in here, the people—the giants who gave us the offset strategy from the 1970s that were so successful didn't wake up every morning with vacuous thoughts about how to transform the force. They woke up trying to solve discrete operational problems of enduring importance: How do I attrit and delay the second echelon of Soviet Army forces in Central Europe in the face of a very robust air defense?

And that is the kind of focused work that can help a strategy like this really make rapid progress toward innovating on the things that our future combatant commanders most need. So that would be step one.

Mr. FORBES. And if I could impose on you——

Mr. OCHMANEK. Yes, sir.

Mr. FORBES [continuing]. Go ahead and take that step. If you were there and you said, "What do we need to be focusing that analysis on?", give me two suggestions that you would put forth.

Mr. OCHMANEK. Two have been mentioned here. One is finding ways that when we project power forward that the forces we project are survivable so that we are not inviting an attack by our adversary, we are not creating targets for him to shoot at.

We don't know how to do that yet. In the 1960s and 1970s, we did it by pouring a lot of concrete at our bases in Germany. It worked well because the adversary didn't have highly accurate weapons. That is not likely to work now.

It is going to be a combination of things: dispersal, getting used to using austere facilities, simple things like rapid runway repair, fuel bladders, things like that. But it is a mix of things, and we have to try it, we have to learn it, we have to practice it. And then we have to resource this.

And, two, again, finding ways to locate, identify, track, engage, damage, and destroy enemy forces on the move in the opening hours of a war. Before we have been able to roll back the air defense, before we have been able to achieve maritime superiority, reaching into that bubble to attack.

Mr. FORBES. So you are looking at more offensive capability than just defensive capability?

Mr. OCHMANEK. I think it is offensive strike capability in the service of a defensive strategy, yes.

Mr. FORBES. Thank you.

Mr. Hunter.

Mr. HUNTER. It is a long list of questions. I think——

Mr. FORBES. Pick two you like.

Mr. HUNTER [continuing]. I got them down.

I would say two assumptions that I think we may have or may make that will be wrong, I think we are wrong if we think we know where the fight will be. I don't think we do know where the fight will be, and we will probably be surprised. That has been a lesson of recent history.

Mr. FORBES. Your former chairman loved to testify that I think he had 13 conflicts while he was here, and 12 of them we did not predict.

Mr. HUNTER. Exactly.

Second—and maybe this is a Pentagon perspective; I am still a recent escapee—is the assumption that regular order is better, better than the alternatives that have been created over the last several years, that we are more insightful when we take a longer period of time to make a decision.

I do think that analysis is critical, and I am not in any way meaning to downplay the importance of it. But our regular-order processes are not holy writ. And there is still a tendency, as we come out of the conflicts that we have been in, as much as we can, over the last 10 years, that if we could just get back to regular order things would work much better. And I think that is a false assumption.

Mr. FORBES. And the two things are not mutually exclusive, you know, to be able to——

Mr. HUNTER. Exactly.

Two next steps. I am going to agree—I know it is a little bit boring, but I am going to agree with Dave on the criticality of experimentation, work on operational concepts, and the net assessment that he mentioned. Those are things that need to be substantially reinforced and upgraded. And, as you know, we changed our structure for engaging in that work in the last several years, and I am not sure it has yet reached a new balance where it ought to be in those capabilities.

And the second step is we need to work with industry, because they are the key to the problem. There is no innovation without talking to industry. And by that, I don't necessarily mean what we think of as the traditional defense industry, the big six contractors of the Department of Defense. I mean industry more broadly. Because it is a global and fully open industry now that is creating the kinds of technologies that are relevant to the problems we are trying to solve.

On how to protect intellectual property, I think you have to look at what industry's incentives are. Although they clearly have a business incentive to protect their intellectual property, they don't necessarily have the incentive to protect it in the way that we would like that to occur. We need to talk to them about what are the incentives that they need to do what we want them to do in regards to their intellectual property.

And then on allies, I think we have to change the culture of the government. This is not just a DOD problem, but there is still a perception that we protect technology by holding it tight. And that is just, I think, not in accord with the reality of a global industrial complex that is out there, that is in the world that we are living in. We can't achieve that goal. And it only inhibits our ability to access technology, the best technology, when that resides in companies that are overseas.

Mr. FORBES. Okay. Thank you.

Mr. Brimley.

Mr. BRIMLEY. Yes, sir. Quickly, I will take on flawed assumptions and next steps.

On flawed assumptions, you will hear echoes of the—me echo the statements of my colleagues.

Number one, that the U.S. will maintain dominance in the guided-weapons regime. As I said in my written statement and my oral statement, I think that assumption is false. I think it is false today. It is certainly going to be false 5, 10, 15 years from now. I think there is an indication—I mean, planners in the Department are moving in this direction, but I think, you know, keeping up that focus in the years ahead will be important.

And, number two, another flawed assumption is that the U.S. will be able to compensate for a loss in the first-mover advantages that one might accrue from being aggressively moving in the unmanned and robotic warfighting regime. I think, given where the intellectual ideas are emanating from, it is not like the 1970s, where it is sort of a DOD-focused S&T [science and technology] R&D. These ideas are emanating—you know, autonomy is happening in Silicon Valley, it is emerging overseas. I worry that we are not going to be able to catch up if we fail to move and move decisively in the next, say, 5 years.

In terms of next steps, I would just encourage Members to make sure that the next budget submission reflects these rhetorical priorities. I think we ought to hold the Pentagon leadership accountable for the rhetorical priorities that it has talked about.

I think we have talked about some program-specific canaries in the coal mine. If you are serious about the offset strategy, here are a couple programs where we can see indications about how the Department is moving. That is going to be very important, I think, in the next 4 to 5 months.

And, number two, just to continue doing what you are doing. I think, for this subcommittee and for the House committee writ large, I would encourage you to develop a year-long series of hearings to fully explore this issue, whether it is a hearing on undersea dominance and payload capacity, a hearing on maritime experimentation, a hearing on alternative air and maritime concepts of operations, where we could start talking about these things more fulsomely in the public domain, and maybe a hearing on what the role of allies and partners is.

And as you pursue, perhaps the allies and partners one is an interesting one. If you call a bunch of defense nerds like us to the table, we will all basically agree with one another. But I think it would be interesting if you called in some regional—some responsible regional players from, say, the Pentagon or the State Department for a hearing like this and really force bridges to be built between, sort of, functional defense expertise in the Department and the more regional policy expertise. That could be a very valuable thing.

Mr. FORBES. Mr. Martinage, we will let you have the last word.

Mr. MARTINAGE. Great. Thank you very much, Congressman Forbes.

On the two flawed assumptions, there are so many, I am not sure where to begin. But the two that I think stick out most to me is the assumption of close-in operational sanctuaries, whether it is airfields, carriers forward, surface combatants forward, airborne tanking forward. We are unlikely to be able to operate that way in the future.

And the second is our freedom of operation, our use of space in the electromagnetic spectrum. I think those are both going to be increasingly contested, with a lot of cascading ramifications for how we think about the joint force and how it operates.

I would echo really what all my colleagues have said on point two—the experimentation, the war-gaming, the conceptual development, I think that is all critical.

And, as Shawn said, while we don't have a crystal ball, I think some near-term wins of things that are put forward under the off-set-strategy umbrella, like the VPM [*Virginia* Payload Module] or UCLASS or directed energy or UUVs and unmanned systems—we are pretty sure that those things are going to figure prominently in the future. You know, we can work out the details later, but I think those are all—would be candidate near-term wins.

In terms of the private sector, I agree on, you know, the importance of bringing them in and, you know, minimizing, you know, espionage and theft. I think the bigger fundamental problem is private industry doesn't really want to work with the Department of Defense, because they put their IP [intellectual property] at risk, their profit margins are constrained, or, you know, they have—very narrow, they have a ton of red tape and regulations to deal with. So, generally speaking, a lot of the cutting-edge R&D that is out there in the private sector, they are not interested in working with the Department of Defense. Which gets back to, you have to fix our acquisition processes in the Department.

And then, lastly, on allies, I think if we come up with a compelling strategy, I think our allies will kind of help us figure out what they can do to support it. I think we need to bring them into the tent as we get this further along. I mean, the process is just starting in the Department. It is probably going to take some months or a year to flesh out the strategy, but I think once we do, I think our allies will want to try to help.

And I think there are likely to be some key roles in command and control, communications, logistics, basing, as well as potentially helping to field and develop some of these new capabilities. Working with some of our closer partners, I think that is possible, as well, to help share some of the burden of doing that.

But, again, I thank you for the opportunity to speak today. Thank you for the subcommittee's interest in this, I think, very important area. And, as Shawn said, I think a series of hearings over the next year or two to keep people's feet to the fire and keeping this on the rails would go a long way.

But thank you.

Mr. FORBES. We thank all of you for your help. As you know, DOD has kind of launched their first volley at this. This is a congressional first volley. And we are going to be doing this for a long time, I am sure, as we try to get our hands around what we need to do and how we need to move forward. So we appreciate your help today, and we are going to continue to try to pick your brains as we move forward.

So, with that—do you have anything else that you have?

With that, thank you, gentlemen, for being here.

And we are adjourned.

[Whereupon, at 5:31 p.m., the subcommittee was adjourned.]

APPENDIX

December 2, 2014

PREPARED STATEMENTS SUBMITTED FOR THE RECORD

December 2, 2014

Opening Remarks of the Honorable J. Randy Forbes,
Chairman of the Seapower and Projection Forces Subcommittee,
for the hearing on
The Role of Maritime and Air Power in DOD's Third Offset Strategy

Today the subcommittee convenes to receive testimony on the role of Seapower and Air Power in DoD's Defense Innovation Initiative (DII) "Offset Strategy."

Our first panel of distinguished guests testifying before us are:

- **Mr. Robert Martinage**
  Senior Fellow
  Center for Strategic and Budgetary Assessments
- **Mr. Shawn Brimley**
  Executive Vice President and Director of Studies
  Center for a New American Security
- **Mr. Andrew Hunter**
  Director, Defense Industrial Initiatives Group and Senior Fellow,
  International Security Program, Center for Strategic and
  International Studies
- **Mr. David Ochmanek**
  RAND Corporation

Gentlemen, thank you for being with us today.

This past summer, Defense Secretary Chuck Hagel concluded in a speech at the Naval War College that "we are entering an era where American dominance…can no longer be taken for granted."

This is a stunning admission that deserves the full and undivided attention of the Congress.

Today, states like China, Russia, Iran, and North Korea are investing in precision-guided munitions, advanced sensors, undersea-warfare, unmanned systems, and offensive cyber and space capabilities to alter the military balance with the United States. Nowhere are these risks more evident that in the Indo-Pacific region, and specifically North East Asia where the People's Republic of

China (PRC) is using its growing economic and military power to coerce its neighbors and challenge the current American-led order. China's investments in what it calls a "counter-intervention" strategy are calling into question our ability to project power, degrading escalation dominance, forcing allies to doubt the credibility of our deterrent, and imposing costs on current joint force capabilities that will make it increasingly difficult to sustain the military edge.

In recent years we have witnessed various response to these emerging challenges, including the establishment of the Air-Sea Battle Office, new weapons programs like the Long-Range Anti-Ship Missile, and operational resiliency initiatives like the Air Force is pursuing in the Pacific. These efforts are all very much necessary, but they illustrate a larger concern: alone and unguided by a true long-range strategic planning process, they are insufficient to prepare the Department of Defense for the future.

When Deputy Secretary of Defense Bob Work began discussing a new "Offset Strategy" this past summer, this subcommittee took notice. I read the available literature on the Offset Strategy of the late 1970s and the "New Look" that Eisenhower initiated in the 1950s and found in this history a useful analogy for today. Just like during these periods, we face new military operational dilemmas that cannot be resolved in our favor by doing more of the same. I believe that the concept of "peace through strength" continues to be a sound maxim for guiding our defense policy. But given the capabilities and new warfighting concepts our competitors are adopting, the answer cannot be to just build *more* military "strength," but to develop and invest in the *right type* of military strength. We need to ask tough questions about the military competitions we find ourselves in, work to match our inherent military advantages and disadvantages against those of our competitors, and invest our time, energy, and resources in new ways to exploit our advantages and shift the military balance back in our favor.

I understand the Department of Defense has initiated a "Defense Innovation Initiative" to develop a new Offset Strategy to prepare the United States for emerging warfighting regimes. While I look forward to future testimony from the Pentagon about this effort, today's hearing provides an opportunity to enhance this subcommittees understanding about the concept of an offset strategy and the potential options the Pentagon can consider in pursuing this new initiative.

Finally, there is one important distinction that I believe needs to be made concerning the Offset Strategy from the 1970s. While there was a tremendous amount of intellectual capital and research & development dollars invested during this period to develop an Offset for Soviet advantages, the resources to fund this effort never materialized. It was not until the Reagan military buildup in the early 1980s that the benefits of capabilities like stealth, precision guided munitions, and sensors could be fielded in a way that actually exploited these new technologies and shifted the military balance in our favor. Today, we face a similar dilemma: absent a reversal of sequestration, we can develop brilliant ideas for a new offset strategy and still will fall short of our objective.

I again thank our panel for being here to testify and look forward to your testimony.

TESTIMONY

December 2, 2014

STATEMENT BEFORE THE HOUSE ARMED SERVICES SUBCOMMITTEE ON SEAPOWER AND PROJECTION FORCES ON THE ROLE OF MARITIME AND AIR POWER IN DOD'S THIRD OFFSET STRATEGY

By Robert Martinage
Senior Fellow
Center for Strategic and Budgetary Assessments

Chairman Forbes, Ranking Member McIntyre, and members of this distinguished Sub-Committee, thank you for the opportunity to share my views on the implications of a "third" offset strategy on air and maritime forces. The Sub-Committee's support and oversight of this issue are crucial. The goal of my testimony today is to draw some lessons from previous offset strategies, explain why a new offset strategy is needed, outline the core elements of such a strategy, and identify near term investment options for implementing it over the coming decades.

As it enters an uncertain period of fiscal austerity, the U.S. military nevertheless confronts a range of worsening security threats around the globe. Preserving U.S. security interests in the face of both exiting and emerging threats is made all the more difficult as traditional sources of U.S. military advantage are being eroded by the maturation and proliferation of disruptive technologies—most notably, anti-access/area denial (A2/AD) capabilities—to state and non-state actors. Absent a major change in how the U.S. military projects power, its ability to deter aggression, reassure allies, and defend U.S. security interests are likely to be increasingly challenged. While China's ongoing military modernization represents the pacing threat in the Asia Pacific, prospective adversaries in other key regions are also acquiring and fielding a wide range of A2/AD capabilities to exploit U.S. vulnerabilities. The trend is clear and disconcerting.

Faced with this multifaceted challenge, the senior leadership of the Department of Defense has called for a new "game-changing offset strategy" akin to President Dwight Eisenhower's "New Look" strategy in the 1950s and Secretary of Defense Harold Brown's "Offset Strategy" in the 1970s. In both instances, the mechanism for "offsetting" the numerical conventional force imbalance relative to the Soviet Union and its satellites was the same: leveraging U.S. technological advantages. In the 1950s, it took the form of increasingly numerous and varied nuclear weapons, long-range delivery systems, and active and passive defenses. Roughly a quarter-century later, the United States made a series of "big bet" investments exploiting the U.S. lead in information technology to revolutionize battlefield command, control, and communications networks; develop more capable tactical surveillance and strike systems to "see deep" and "shoot deep" into Warsaw Pact territory; exploit space for precision navigation, communications, and reconnaissance; and apply stealth technologies to combat aircraft.

While it is unlikely that a disruptive U.S. capability advantage comparable to that conferred by nuclear weapons in the wake of World War II is in the offing, four important lessons with contemporary applicability to the projection of air and maritime power can be discerned from the New Look in the 1950s. First, and most importantly, is the need for a strategy that provides U.S. leaders with options that can be tailored to address a wide range of anticipated threats. While this lesson may ostensibly seem at odds with the "massive retaliation" moniker often coupled with the New Look, it should not be forgotten that NSC 162/2 also called for "ready forces of the United States and its allies suitably deployed and adequate to deter or initially to counter aggression." Nuclear weapons provided a cost-effective "backstop" for outnumbered conventional forces—not a wholesale replacement for them. Second, the global air warfare capability that emerged from the New Look—and remains a key source of U.S. competitive advantage today—provided valuable strategic freedom of maneuver, complicating the Soviet Union's defensive planning while reducing basing vulnerability. Third, the threat of asymmetric punishment—the capability and willingness to strike outside the theater of operations chosen by an adversary with flexible means—can further increase an adversary's uncertainty, enhancing deterrence. Lastly, alliances matter—not only for burden sharing, but also for complicating an adversary's operational planning and imposing costs upon them.

Relevant lessons can also be drawn from Secretary Brown's "Offset Strategy" during the 1970s. First, technology can multiply the combat effectiveness of a smaller force such that it "offsets" a larger, but technically inferior, force. Second, rather than competing "jet for jet" or "missile for missile," capability advantages can be used to shape the competition, shifting it into areas where the U.S. military can compete more effectively. Third, it is important to retain sufficient "low-end" capabilities to maintain an affordable forward-deployed, combat-credible presence around the globe to deter and, if necessary, respond to contingencies short of high-end, major combat operations. The final lesson from this period is the importance of strategic continuity and institutional commitment. While DoD initiated several technology development programs in the late 1970s, they never would have been fielded if not for enduring bureaucratic support in the Pentagon, in successive presidential administrations, and on Capitol Hill.

These lessons have great value as we consider the situation facing the United States today. The U.S. military has enjoyed a near monopoly in the precision-strike revolution ushered in by the second offset strategy for nearly a quarter-century, but it is beginning to fade away. Prospective adversaries are fielding their own

---

34

reconnaissance-strike networks—battle networks linked to extended-range precision strike forces—to challenge the U.S. approach to power projection. Consequently, the U.S. military now faces four core operational problems:

1. Close-in regional bases (e.g., ports, airfields, and ground installations) are increasingly vulnerable to attack in a growing number of countries around the world;
2. Large surface combatants and aircraft carriers at sea are becoming easier to detect, track, and engage at extended range from an adversary's coast;
3. Non-stealthy aircraft are becoming more vulnerable to being shot down by modern integrated air defense networks; and
4. Space is no longer a sanctuary from attack.

These growing operational challenges have problematic strategic ramifications: heightened crisis instability; declining credibility of U.S. deterrence threats and allied confidence in the U.S. military's ability to meet its security commitments; and increasing cost imposition on the United States, undermining its ability to compete with prospective rivals over time.

Given the increasing scale and diversity of these global threats, trying to counter them symmetrically with tailored forces, or competing "missile for missile" is likely to be both futile and (given current budget projections) unaffordable over the long run. The United States cannot afford to simply scale up the current mix of joint power projection capabilities. Indeed, owing to ballooning personnel costs, especially with respect to medical care and retirement, manpower levels will likely shrink over the coming decades. Similarly, while active defenses and countermeasures may be tactically effective and operationally useful in some circumstances, they must not be allowed to crowd out offensive capability and capacity, which is the foundation upon which deterrence is built.

What is needed, therefore, is a new offset strategy for projecting power effectively and affordably across the threat spectrum. While it must take account of America's fiscal circumstances, its central purpose must be to address the most pressing military challenge that we face: maintaining our ability to project power globally to deter potential adversaries and reassure allies and friends despite the emergence of A2/AD threats. This can be achieved by leveraging U.S. "core competencies" in unmanned systems and automation, extended-range and low-observable air operations, undersea warfare, and complex system engineering and integration to enable new operational concepts for projecting power. As used here, a core competency is defined as a complex combination of technology, the industrial base, skilled manpower, training, doctrine, and practical experience that enables the U.S.

military to conduct strategically useful operations that are difficult for rivals to duplicate or counter. [1]

U.S. conventional deterrence credibility would also be enhanced by adopting a strategy that is less dependent upon the threat to restore the status quo ante through the direct application of force against an adversary's fielded forces. Instead, the United States should focus more on decreasing an adversary's perception of the probability of achieving its war aims in the first place (i.e., deterrence by denial) and increasing the anticipated costs of attempting to do so by threatening asymmetric retaliatory attacks (i.e., deterrence by punishment). The former would require both a high degree of situational awareness and the ability to apply force quickly to derail an adversary's campaign in its opening phases, regardless of the threat situation or basing availability. It would, therefore, put a premium on survivable forces that can operate within an enemy's A2/AD envelope persistently and effectively. Examples of these kinds of forces include undersea platforms and fast, long-range stealthy aircraft. The latter would require the ability to identify and destroy high-value targets regardless of where they are located or how they are defended, which would place a premium on survivability and lethality.

As part of a new offset strategy, the above-mentioned U.S. capability advantages (i.e., unmanned systems and automation, extended-range and low-observable air operations, undersea warfare, and complex system engineering and integration) could provide the foundation for a global surveillance and strike (GSS) network that would be:

- Balanced, in that it would comprise a mix of low-end and high-end platforms aligned to widely varying threat environments—including advanced A2/AD challenges;

- Resilient, in that it would be geographically distributed with less dependence upon close-in bases, have greatly reduced sensitivity to enemy air defense capabilities, and be significantly more tolerant of disruptions to space-based systems;

- Responsive, in that a credible surveillance-strike presence could be generated within hours of the direction to do so by taking advantage of rapid global reach and survivable forward presence; and

- Scalable, in that it could by expanded to influence events in multiple locations around the world concurrently.

While many elements of the U.S. military would have important roles to play in a future GSS network, it would emphasize air and maritime forces capable of operating far forward in denied areas largely independent of support forces or close-in bases. In particular, it would leverage autonomous unmanned systems,

---

[1] W. Cockell, J. J. Martin, and G. Weaver, *Core Competencies and Other Business Concepts for Use in DoD Strategic Planning* (McLean, VA: SAIC, February 7, 1992). This report was done for the Directors of Net Assessment, OSD, and the Defense Nuclear Agency.

given their advantages in terms of ultra-long mission endurance and low life-cycle costs relative to manned platforms.

A family of concepts for employing combinations of new and legacy air and maritime forces, complemented by other joint capabilities, could be developed under the GSS umbrella for addressing potential operational challenges posed by specific adversaries. In the event that deterrence failed, GSS forces could quickly mount strikes against fixed, mobile, hardened, and deep inland targets to thwart an aggressor's war aims; conduct asymmetric "punishment" campaigns, if necessary, against multiple adversaries concurrently; and, if required, set the stage for a large-scale, multi-phased, combined arms campaign by "rolling back" an adversary's A2/AD defenses.

To realize the GSS concept, the Department of Defense should consider undertaking the following actions:

- Increase space resiliency by, for example, developing cost-effective counters to adversarial anti-satellite systems or disaggregating payloads on both commercial and military satellites;

- Hedge against the loss of space-based enablers by accelerating R&D on alternatives to GPS for precision navigation and timing, fielding a "high-low" mix of unmanned surveillance aircraft with long mission endurance and/or aerial refueling capability, and developing an "aerial layer" alternative to space for long-haul communications;

- Develop and make known counter-space capabilities, especially those capable of achieving reversible effects, to deter prospective adversaries from attacking U.S. satellites;

- Expand the geographic coverage of the undersea fleet by accelerating development of key enabling technologies for unmanned undersea vehicles (UUVs) including high-density energy storage for power and endurance, undersea navigation and communications, and autonomy;

- Expand undersea payload capacity by both increasing available volume onboard future submarines and fielding a family of external payload modules that could be clandestinely pre-deployed into forward operating areas;

- Increase submarine payload flexibility by developing non-kinetic weapons (e.g., undersea-launched airborne jammers and decoys), modifying existing missiles to address a wider array of target sets, and initiating development of a submarine-launched, conventional ballistic/boost-glide missile;

- Expand geographic coverage provided by fixed and deployable undersea sensor networks;

- Develop and field modern ground-, air-, and sea-deployed naval mines, as well as a long-range anti-submarine warfare weapon;

- Reverse the active defense versus missile attack cost exchange ratio that currently strongly favors the offense by accelerating development and fielding of electromagnetic railguns and directed-energy systems;
- Develop and field new counter-sensor weapons including directed-energy systems (e.g., high-power microwave payloads and high-energy lasers) and stand-in jammers/decoys;
- Accelerate fielding of aerial refueling capabilities while seeking opportunities to increase automation;
- Continue developing and fielding the long-range strike bomber;
- Develop and field a land-based, penetrating, high-altitude, long-endurance UAV for medium-high threat environments;
- Develop and field penetrating, air-refuelable land- and carrier-based unmanned combat air systems optimized for distributed surveillance-strike operations (i.e., mobile-relocatable target killers) in medium-high threat environments; and
- Develop expeditionary, ground-based, local "A2/AD" networks comprising short-to-medium range air defenses, coastal defense cruise missiles, defensive mines and UUVs, and mobile surface-to-surface missiles.

Such initiatives would contribute to an effective offset strategy by restoring U.S. power projection capability and capacity and bolstering conventional deterrence by supporting a credible threat of denial and punishment. It also has the potential for imposing disproportionate costs upon prospective adversaries as part of a long-term competition by devaluing large enemy "sunk cost" investments, in part by channeling competition into areas (e.g., undersea warfare) where the United States can compete more effectively or areas that are less threatening from a U.S. perspective.

To fund development of these and other high-payoff capabilities, DoD should redouble efforts to reduce spending on "tail" as opposed to "tooth" by shedding excess basing infrastructure in the continental United States, restructuring the personnel system to reduce ballooning medical and retirement costs, and reforming ossified and inefficient acquisition processes. In addition, selected allies (e.g., Australia, Japan, and the United Kingdom) might be willing to share costs associated with the development, procurement, and operation of some GSS capabilities. Allies might also be will to take on additional responsibility for key enabling functions, such as survivable basing, logistics support, and communications.

Given the intensifying global threat and need to "offset" the proliferation of A2/AD networks with high-payoff investments in areas of enduring U.S. advantage, a strong case can also be made for rescinding the Budget Control Act of 2011 and restoring defense funding to the level reflected in the FY 2012 "Gates" budget, also recommended by the bipartisan National Defense Panel. This would restore an average of nearly $100 billion per year to the Pentagon over the next decade. DoD also needs to rebalance the current defense investment portfolio to put relatively more emphasis on capabilities for projecting power into medium and high threat environments. Reducing force structure and scaling back modernization plans for forces that contribute primarily to operations in more permissive threat environments necessarily means having less capacity for some contingencies. The magnitude of such cutbacks and associated risk would largely be a function of the level of funding that Congress restores to the Department of Defense. Regardless of the budget, however, it is imperative to rectify the growing imbalance between forces able to operate in permissive versus non-permissive environments.

Just as it took well over a decade to field every "assault breaker" capability envisioned in the mid-1970s, the GSS network would not attain an initial operational capability until the mid-2020s, but only if focused R&D begins now and the Pentagon, the White House, and Capitol Hill stay the course over successive administrations. A sustained wargaming program across the Department is also needed to develop and refine novel operational and force employment concepts.

Given current constraints on resources for defense, the nation can neither afford to continue the current "business-as-usual" approach to power projection, nor plan on having the resources and time to rectify the many operational and strategic problems inherent on the current path once they fully manifest. Congress needs to be an active partner in restoring and sustaining U.S. air and maritime power projection capacity over the coming decades through the formulation and implementation of a third offset strategy.

About the Center for Strategic and Budgetary Assessments

The Center for Strategic and Budgetary Assessments (CSBA) is an independent, nonpartisan policy research institute established to promote innovative thinking and debate about national security strategy and investment options. CSBA's analysis focuses on key questions related to existing and emerging threats to U.S. national security, and its goal is to enable policymakers to make informed decisions on matters of strategy, security policy, and resource allocation.

Robert Martinage

Senior Fellow

Mr. Martinage recently returned to CSBA after five years of public service in the Department of Defense (DoD). While performing the duties of the Under Secretary of Navy, he led development of the Department of the Navy's FY 2014/2015 budgets and represented the Department during the Strategic Choices and Management Review, as well as within the Defense Management Action Group (DMAG). From 2010-2013, Mr. Martinage served as the Deputy Under Secretary of the Navy, providing senior-level advice on foreign and defense policy, naval capability and readiness, security policy, intelligence oversight, and special programs. Appointed Principal Deputy Assistant Secretary of Defense for Special Operations, Low-Intensity Conflict and Interdependent Capabilities in the Office of the Secretary of Defense (OSD) in 2009, Mr. Martinage focused on special operations, irregular warfare, counter-terrorism, and security force assistance policy. He also led a two-year, DoD-wide effort to develop an investment path for a future long-range strike "family of systems."

Prior to his government service, Mr. Martinage was employed at CSBA where he was responsible for carrying out a broad research program on defense strategy and planning, military modernization, and future warfare for government, foundation, and corporate clients. He has more than 14 years of experience designing, conducting, and analyzing over 40 wargames and numerous studies focused on conventional operations in high-end threat environments, special operations, irregular warfare, and strategic deterrence and warfare.

Mr. Martinage holds a MA from The Fletcher School of Law & Diplomacy with concentrations in International Security Studies, Southwest Asia, International Negotiation & Conflict Resolution, and Civilization & Foreign Affairs. Mr. Martinage earned his BA cum laude from Dartmouth College in Government with concentrations in International Relations and Political Theory & Public Law.

DISCLOSURE FORM FOR WITNESSES
CONCERNING FEDERAL CONTRACT AND GRANT INFORMATION

INSTRUCTION TO WITNESSES: Rule 11, clause 2(g)(5), of the Rules of the U.S. House of Representatives for the 113th Congress requires nongovernmental witnesses appearing before House committees to include in their written statements a curriculum vitae and a disclosure of the amount and source of any federal contracts or grants (including subcontracts and subgrants) received during the current and two previous fiscal years either by the witness or by an entity represented by the witness. This form is intended to assist witnesses appearing before the House Committee on Armed Services in complying with the House rule. Please note that a copy of these statements, with appropriate redactions to protect the witness's personal privacy (including home address and phone number) will be made publicly available in electronic form not later than one day after the witness's appearance before the committee.

Witness name: Robert Martinage

Capacity in which appearing: (check one)

_X__ Individual

___ Representative

If appearing in a representative capacity, name of the company, association or other entity being represented:

FISCAL YEAR 2014

federal grant(s) / contracts	federal agency	dollar value	subject(s) of contract or grant
WHS	DOD/ONA	$1,364,000	Assessments/analysis, wargames, and briefings on international security environment, strategic challenges, future warfare, and portfolio rebalancing
DLA Acquisition Directorate	National Defense University	$87,000	Secretary of Defense Corporate Fellows Program Orientation
MOBIS	Department of the Navy	$121,000	Portfolio rebalancing

FISCAL YEAR 2013

federal grant(s) / contracts	federal agency	dollar value	subject(s) of contract or grant
WHS	DOD/ONA	$1,200,000	Assessments/analysis, wargames, and briefings on international security environment, strategic

41

			challenges, future warfare, and portfolio rebalancing
DLA Acquisition Directorate	National Defense University	$84,000	Secretary of Defense Corporate Fellows Program Orientation
MOBIS	Army War College	$121,000	Portfolio rebalancing
MOBIS	National Commission on the Structure of the Air Force	$75,000	Portfolio rebalancing
DARPA	DARPA	$175,000	Research and analysis

FISCAL YEAR 2012

Federal grant(s) / contracts	federal agency	dollar value	subject(s) of contract or grant
WHS	DOD/ONA	$1,800,000	Assessments/analysis, wargames, and briefings on international security environment, strategic challenges, future warfare, and portfolio rebalancing
DLA Acquisition Directorate	National Defense University	$80,000	Secretary of Defense Corporate Fellows Program Orientation
CTTSO SETA	OASD (SO/LIC)	551,000	Future requirements and visioning

Federal Contract Information: If you or the entity you represent before the Committee on Armed Services has contracts (including subcontracts) with the federal government, please provide the following information:

Number of contracts (including subcontracts) with the federal government:

Current fiscal year (2014):_____3_____;
Fiscal year 2013:_____5_____;
Fiscal year 2012:_____3_____.

Federal agencies with which federal contracts are held:

Current fiscal year (2014):_____3_____;
Fiscal year 2013:_____4_____;
Fiscal year 2012:_____2_____.

List of subjects of federal contract(s) (for example, ship construction, aircraft parts manufacturing, software design, force structure consultant, architecture & engineering services, etc.):

Current fiscal year (2014):___Research and analysis_____;
Fiscal year 2013:_____Research and analysis_____;
Fiscal year 2012:_____Research and analysis_____.

Aggregate dollar value of federal contracts held:

Current fiscal year (2014): ___$1,572,000_____;
Fiscal year 2013:_____$1,655,000_____;
Fiscal year 2012: _____$2,431,000_____.

Federal Grant Information: If you or the entity you represent before the Committee on Armed Services has grants (including subgrants) with the federal government, please provide the following information:

Number of grants (including subgrants) with the federal government:

> Current fiscal year (2014):_____;
> Fiscal year 2013:_____;
> Fiscal year 2012:_____.

Federal agencies with which federal grants are held:

> Current fiscal year (2014):_____;
> Fiscal year 2013:_____;
> Fiscal year 2012:_____.

List of subjects of federal grants(s) (for example, materials research, sociological study, software design, etc.):

> Current fiscal year (2014):_____;
> Fiscal year 2013:_____;
> Fiscal year 2012:_____.

Aggregate dollar value of federal grants held:

> Current fiscal year (2014):_____;
> Fiscal year 2013:_____;
> Fiscal year 2012:_____.

Statement of Shawn W. Brimley
Before the House Armed Services Committee
Subcommittee on Seapower and Projection Forces
Hearing on the Role of Maritime and Air Power in DoD's Third Offset Strategy
December 2, 2014

The Third Offset Strategy: Securing America's Military-Technical Advantage

Thank you Chairman Forbes and Ranking Member McIntyre for the opportunity to testify and submit this written statement for the record.[1]

Today's headlines are reinforcing the alarms sounded by defense policymakers and analysts warning of the perils of cuts to the defense budget, the blind meat-axe of sequestration, and the risks to America's global position. From the spread of the Islamic State in Iraq and the Levant (ISIL), to Russia's aggression in Crimea and eastern Ukraine, to China's slow but steady push into contested areas of the East and South China Seas, the United States seems to be on its heels.

But there is a deeper competition afoot, one that goes beyond the daily tactical game of foreign policy maneuvering and diplomatic talking points. It is a strategic competition played out over decades, and it's one that the United States could very well lose. It is a competition that most national security figures and the broader mainstream media don't seem to fully grasp. It's a contest over military-technical superiority, and whether the United States can sustain its advantage deep into the 21st century or be overtaken by its competitors.

What does "military-technical superiority" mean and why does that matter? Simply put, America's national security depends on our military being more technically advanced than any other. America's armed forces must project and sustain power across oceans and be able to perform complex offensive and defensive operations in all types of geographic terrain and in all operating domains. No other nation state requires this kind of global power projection capability to adequately protect its national interests—the United States is unique in this regard. This ability is a critical element of U.S. national security strategy and is foundational to the sustainment of U.S. military power and influence. But after over 25 years of U.S. power projection being a source of unique advantage, today it forms the basis for a long-term military competition.

To understand why this competition is so important, one needs to focus on the core context in which military competitions have played out over history. There have only been two basic warfighting paradigms or "regimes" in history: the "unguided weapons regime" and the "guided weapons regime." The unguided weapons regime was the world of stones, arrows, machine guns, artillery, and bombs. The key characteristic of combat using unguided, ballistic munitions—even over relatively short ranges—was that most munitions that were thrown, shot,

---

[1] This statement draws extensively from the following article: Shawn Brimley, "Offset Strategies and Warfighting Regimes," *War on the Rocks* (October 15, 2014): http://warontherocks.com/2014/10/offset-strategies-warfighting-regimes/.

[2] William Perry, "Technology and National Security: Risks and Responsibilities," Speech at France-Stanford Center for Interdisciplinary Studies, April 7-8 2003: http://stanford.edu/dept/france-stanford/Conferences/Risk/Perry.pdf

fired, launched, or dropped *ultimately missed their targets*. Therefore, in order to maximize success at the point of attack, commanders would often seek to aggregate their forces in order to achieve numerical superiority. *As a result, unguided weapons warfare had an inherent bias toward mass.*

The crucible of World War II and the early Cold War period drove the development of two alternative ways for the United States to compensate or *offset* the numerical advantages our adversaries often enjoyed.

The first offset strategy centered on atomic weapons. The massive destructive power inherent in a nuclear blast obviated the need for much accuracy. One didn't need to use more than one nuclear weapon to be assured of a devastating effect on the target. This was initially attractive to the United States as a means to compensate for insufficient land forces in Europe. But in the early Cold War, the difficulties of actually contemplating how to employ tactical nuclear weapons on the battlefield vexed military planners. And as the Soviets approached basic parity in the nuclear balance, the advantage the United States enjoyed faded quickly. As former Secretary of Defense William Perry has written: "...by the mid-1970s, NATO and the United States were looking at a Soviet Union with parity in nuclear weapons and about a 3-fold advantage in conventional weapons. Many in the United States began to fear that this development threatened deterrence."[2] This fear drove the search for a new way to offset Soviet military power.

The second offset strategy that reduced the need for mass on the battlefield came in the form of guided conventional weapons that actively corrected their trajectories after being fired, released, or launched. From their introduction late in World War II up through the end of the 20th century, the main driver of U.S. military-technical superiority has been the development and effective employment of guided munitions. Other transformative technologies like stealth, the global positioning system and the broader revolution in computer networking acted as critical means to an end—the employment of guided weapons. Put simply, guided weapons ushered in an entirely new era in warfare, one in which *accuracy became independent of range.*[3]

This was a key strategic element in answering the challenge posed by the Soviet Union, who enjoyed clear quantitative superiority in Europe. Soviet military leaders understood (sooner than their U.S. counterparts) that their entire operational concept of overwhelming NATO forces with sheer mass would no longer be effective given the American lead in fielding guided weapons.[4] By the mid-1980s Soviet military theorists had concluded that the emerging U.S. "reconnaissance-strike complexes" would be able to achieve destructive effects similar to tactical nuclear weapons. Put another way, because the United States leveraged its broader technical

---

[2] William Perry, "Technology and National Security: Risks and Responsibilities," Speech at France-Stanford Center for Interdisciplinary Studies, April 7-8 2003: http://stanford.edu/dept/france-stanford/Conferences/Risk/Perry.pdf

[3] The emergence of guided munitions and associated battle networks changed the characteristics of modern warfare. "...when firing munitions blessed with accuracy independent of range, forces could now mass effects by fire from greater distances while operating from a dispersed posture, using far less ammunition... [I]n collisions between conventional forces, a smaller force employing guided weapons might be capable of defeating a much larger force that employed unguided ones." See Robert O. Work and Shawn Brimley, *20YY: Preparing for War in the Robotic Age* (Washington DC: Center for a New American Security, January 2014).

[4] See Barry Watts, *The Evolution of Precision Strike* (Washington DC: Center for Strategic and Budgetary Assessments, 2013).

prowess to develop a way to *offset* Soviet military advantage, the basic structure of the entire Cold War military competition shifted to U.S. advantage.

The lesson here is clear. When technologies emerge that upend the dominant warfighting paradigm, or "regime," they can significantly alter the course of history. Eliminate the advent of guided conventional weapons and the history of the 20[th]century would look very different indeed. This is why defense analysts have such reverence for figures like former Secretary of Defense William Perry: He played a critical role in the late 1970s (as Undersecretary of Defense for Research and Engineering), by driving the Department of Defense toward increased investments in guided munitions and their associated battle networks.[5] Had Perry and his colleagues not invested in these emerging and sometimes unproven technologies, the last decade of the Cold War might have unfolded in very different (and potentially violent) ways.

Since the end of the Cold War, the United States has continued to benefit from its initial first-mover advantages in what has become the "guided-munitions regime." The United States made the first and largest investments in these technologies and has continued to reap those rewards to the benefit of America's national interests and defense strategy. But there is good reason to think that the advantages accrued from the Cold War offset strategy have largely run their course. Deputy Secretary of Defense Robert O. Work outlined in August 2014 why the offset strategy of the late Cold War – the move toward the guided weapons regime – is no longer a sound basis for defense strategy and force development. He explained:

> *While the United States fought two lengthy wars, the rest of the world did not sit idly by, they saw what our advantages were back in 1991s Desert Storm, they studied them, and they set about devising ways to compete. Today, many of those earlier innovations that were spurred by the intense military-technical competition with the Soviet Union – in missilery, space systems, guided munitions, stealth, and battle networking – have proliferated widely. Unsophisticated militaries and non-state actors are seeking and acquiring destructive technologies and weapons that were once the province of advanced militaries – and the price of acquiring these weapons is dropping.[6]*

In a speech to a defense industry audience in September, Secretary Hagel made a similar argument to Work's, and went further:

> *...Meanwhile, China and Russia have been trying to close the technology gap by pursuing and funding long-term, comprehensive military modernization programs. They are also developing anti-ship, anti-air, counter-space, cyber, electronic warfare, and special operations capabilities that appear designed to counter traditional U.S. military advantages – in particular, our ability to project power to any region across the globe by surging aircraft, ships, troops, and supplies.[7]*

---

[5] See William J. Perry, "Desert Storm and Deterrence," *Foreign Affairs* (Fall 1991).
[6] Robert O. Work, *Speech at National Defense University* (August 5, 2014).
[7] Secretary of Defense Chuck Hagel, *Speech to Southeastern New England Defense Industry Alliance* (September 3, 2014).

"All this suggests," Hagel concluded, "that we are entering an era where American dominance on the seas, in the skies, and in space – not to mention cyberspace – can no longer be taken for granted."

Hagel and Work are essentially arguing that our first-mover advantage in the shift to guided weapons has almost fully played itself out. We are approaching a world in which the guided munitions regime is fully mature, with a much broader range of players now fully invested. U.S. defense planners must now assume that future adversaries will employ sophisticated battle networks and advanced guided munitions to both deter and defeat U.S. military forces. We see this dynamic most clearly with respect to the military competition unfolding in Asia.

China's military modernization is entirely focused on moving decisively, and asymmetrically, into the guided weapons regime. So while the United States faces many plausible defense challenges, to the degree that military planners worry about what war looks like in a world of guided munitions, China is most certainly a "pacing threat"—that is, an actor that is making the most progress toward plausibly contesting U.S. defense strategy in a particularly worrisome way. It is true that other actors—Russia, Iran, North Korea, and even non-state groups like Hezbollah—are also fielding guided munitions and could employ them in creative ways to undermine U.S. military operations, but China is leading the pack. Therefore it is reasonable for defense planners to focus on the kinds of operational challenges the People's Liberation Army may pose, as the underlying technologies will rapidly proliferate to other actors.[8]

If the emerging consensus is correct that the Cold War offset strategy—embracing the shift to guided weapons—is no longer a sufficient means to sustain U.S. military-technical advantage, what then can serve as a basis for prudent defense strategy and force development efforts? This is clearly the question Hagel and Work have asked of Pentagon planners. "As we see [U.S. military-technical] advantages begin to erode," Hagel said in his Newport speech, "I've asked Bob [Work] to move forward with an initiative to develop a third, game-changing offset strategy." He identified Under Secretary of Defense for Acquisition, Technology, and Logistics, Frank Kendall as the point person for "assuring our technological edge through the next several decades" and announced plans for a new Long-Range Research & Development Planning Program to work towards that goal.

The name of this initiative—the Long-Range Research & Development Planning Program (LRRDPP)—is notable, as it is exactly the same as the task force William Perry stood up in the late 1970s that led to the United States moving decidedly into the guided weapons regime.

But how should the new LRRDPP proceed? In order to properly begin to develop a new offset strategy it is critical that the Pentagon resist the powerful temptation to think first about technologies and then about strategy. Officials must first be very clear about the military problem they are attempting to solve. To me, the basic question is something like the following: How will the U.S. military deter and defeat an adversary that has guided munitions parity?

---

[8] See Michael Horowitz, *The Diffusion of Military Power: Causes and Consequences for International Politics* (Princeton University Press, 2010).

Components of an answer would need to explore many issues, such as how to defend against long-range guided munitions at favorable cost-exchange ratios, ensure U.S. aircraft carriers can project strike power beyond adversary missile ranges, and maintain resilience in our own guided munitions and battle networks as plausible adversaries develop ways to contest and degrade U.S. command-and-control links. Dominance in emerging areas of competition will also be crucial, particularly those powered by information technology. Superiority in cyberspace is likely to be a prerequisite to successful military operations in other domains.

I suspect that a critical component of addressing the challenges our forces will face in an era of guided munitions parity will revolve around fully harnessing the possibilities inherent in unmanned and increasingly autonomous (robotic) systems. From a certain perspective, guided munitions are very simple robotic systems.[9] Over time, as computing power increases, the "smarts" behind smart weapons will grow. We have only scratched the surface of what unmanned and increasingly autonomous systems will make possible. Robotics is also another area where commercial and industrial investment outpaces military spending, requiring a different model for staying ahead. Unlike microprocessor technology of the 1970s, the underlying technologies behind advanced robotics will be widely available, meaning the Department of Defense must have the ability to rapidly import commercial sector innovations and quickly develop new concepts of operation for employing robotic systems.

There are undoubtedly many issues that Pentagon planners — and the defense community more broadly — ought to tackle as part of developing a new offset strategy. Beyond fully exploiting unmanned and autonomous systems, we need to determine how to employ emerging technologies like directed energy (critical for sustainable defense against salvos of guided missiles) and improved power systems and storage (to harness the potential of robotic systems to stay in the air or under the ocean for long periods of time).

There are also critical strategy and policy questions that must be integrated into Pentagon efforts. As one example, officials must not forget that the offset strategy of the late 1970s had two key components: identifying and investing in emerging game-changing technologies; and ensuring these technologies did not fall in Soviet hands.[10] Much of today's military export-control regulations stem from a Cold War-era desire to prevent U.S. technologies from proliferating. Like the Cold War offset strategy, today's effort needs to identify and invest in emerging technologies. But, unlike the offset strategy of the late 1970s, the Pentagon needs to focus on ensuring that more of our capabilities are accessible to key U.S. allies and partners. In a world where advanced technologies are widely available and proliferating rapidly, the United States requires a more liberal approach to exporting defense technologies.

---

[9] I thank my CNAS colleague Paul Scharre for this insight. See also Scharre's recent CNAS reports, *Robotics on the Battlefield: Range Persistence and Daring* (May 2014) and also *Robotics on the Battlefield: The Coming Swarm* (October 2014).

[10] Former Deputy Secretary of Defense Ash Carter has written that the Cold War-era offset strategy had two components: "The first was to field superior technology through aggressive pursuit of military R&D, and developing a high-technology defense industrial base. The second was to deny opponents that technology through a system of export controls and protection of technological secrets." See Ash Carter, "Keeping the Technological Edge," in *Keeping the Edge: Managing Defense for the Future*, Ash Carter and John White (eds), (Cambridge MA: MIT Press, 2000).

Another strategy question to integrate into the LRRDPP effort is examining how the technologies under consideration might affect what analysts call "crisis stability." For instance, one important implication of the guided weapons regime is that it favors offensive warfare, as defending against long-range precision strikes is extremely difficult. This makes the developing military tensions in the Asia-Pacific all the more concerning. As actors like China approach (or perceive themselves to be approaching) something like guided munitions parity with the United States, it may create a "use or lose" dynamic with respect to each actor's precision munitions and battle networks. This dynamic will get worse as more actors in Asia invest in guided munitions and maintaining crisis stability becomes far more difficult. We must explore and plan for the strategic implications of the force development efforts that a "third offset strategy" will spur.

The challenges associated with developing a new strategy to secure U.S. military-technical superiority are many. Budgets are tight, resources scarce, and defenders of the status quo have strong constituencies. Given the top-cover established by the Pentagon's senior leadership however, I am optimistic that Pentagon planners and the broader defense community are poised to articulate a vision of military-technical supremacy that will guide U.S. defense strategy and force development in the decades ahead.

Shawn Brimley
Executive Vice President and Director of Studies
Center for a New American Security

Shawn Brimley is Executive Vice President and Director of Studies at the Center for a New American Security (CNAS). Mr. Brimley served in the Obama Administration from February 2009 to October 2012 most recently as Director for Strategic Planning on the National Security Council staff at the White House. He also served as Special Advisor to the Under Secretary of Defense for Policy at the Pentagon from 2009 to 2011, where he focused on the 2010 Quadrennial Defense Review, overseas basing and posture, and long-range strategy development. He has been awarded the Secretary of Defense Medal for Outstanding Public Service and the Office of the Secretary of Defense Medal for Exceptional Public Service. Mr. Brimley was a founding member of CNAS in 2007 and was the inaugural recipient of the 1Lt. Andrew Bacevich Jr. Memorial Fellowship. He has also worked at the Center for Strategic and International Studies.

Mr. Brimley has published widely, including in the *New York Times, Foreign Affairs* and *Foreign Policy*. Educated at Queen's University and George Washington University, Mr. Brimley is a term member of the Council on Foreign Relations. He lives in Washington with his wife and their three children.

DISCLOSURE FORM FOR WITNESSES
CONCERNING FEDERAL CONTRACT AND GRANT INFORMATION

INSTRUCTION TO WITNESSES: Rule 11, clause 2(g)(5), of the Rules of the U.S. House of Representatives for the 113th Congress requires nongovernmental witnesses appearing before House committees to include in their written statements a curriculum vitae and a disclosure of the amount and source of any federal contracts or grants (including subcontracts and subgrants) received during the current and two previous fiscal years either by the witness or by an entity represented by the witness. This form is intended to assist witnesses appearing before the House Committee on Armed Services in complying with the House rule. Please note that a copy of these statements, with appropriate redactions to protect the witness's personal privacy (including home address and phone number) will be made publicly available in electronic form not later than one day after the witness's appearance before the committee.

Witness name: Shawn Brimley

Capacity in which appearing: (check one)

_X_ Individual

____Representative

If appearing in a representative capacity, name of the company, association or other entity being represented:

FISCAL YEAR 2014

federal grant(s) / contracts	federal agency	dollar value	subject(s) of contract or grant
None			

FISCAL YEAR 2013

federal grant(s) / contracts	federal agency	dollar value	subject(s) of contract or grant
None			

52

FISCAL YEAR 2012

Federal grant(s) / contracts	federal agency	dollar value	subject(s) of contract or grant
None			

Federal Contract Information: If you or the entity you represent before the Committee on Armed Services has contracts (including subcontracts) with the federal government, please provide the following information:

Number of contracts (including subcontracts) with the federal government:

      Current fiscal year (2014):___None_____;
      Fiscal year 2013:_____None _____;
      Fiscal year 2012:_____None_____.

Federal agencies with which federal contracts are held:

      Current fiscal year (2014):___None_____;
      Fiscal year 2013:_____None _____;
      Fiscal year 2012:_____None_____.

List of subjects of federal contract(s) (for example, ship construction, aircraft parts manufacturing, software design, force structure consultant, architecture & engineering services, etc.):

      Current fiscal year (2014):___None_____;
      Fiscal year 2013:_____None _____;
      Fiscal year 2012:_____None_____.

Aggregate dollar value of federal contracts held:

      Current fiscal year (2014):___None_____;
      Fiscal year 2013:_____None _____;
      Fiscal year 2012:_____None_____.

Federal Grant Information: If you or the entity you represent before the Committee on Armed Services has grants (including subgrants) with the federal government, please provide the following information:

Number of grants (including subgrants) with the federal government:

   Current fiscal year (2014):___None_____;
   Fiscal year 2013:_____None _____;
   Fiscal year 2012:_____None_____.

Federal agencies with which federal grants are held:

   Current fiscal year (2014):___None_____;
   Fiscal year 2013:_____None _____;
   Fiscal year 2012:_____None_____.

List of subjects of federal grants(s) (for example, materials research, sociological study, software design, etc.):

   Current fiscal year (2014):___None_____;
   Fiscal year 2013:_____None _____;
   Fiscal year 2012:_____None_____.

Aggregate dollar value of federal grants held:

   Current fiscal year (2014):___None_____;
   Fiscal year 2013:_____None _____;
   Fiscal year 2012:_____None_____.

Statement before the U.S. House of Representatives Committee on Armed Services

Subcommittee on Seapower and Projection Forces

"THE ROLE OF MARITIME AND AIR POWER IN DOD'S THIRD OFFSET STRATEGY"

A Statement by

Andrew Hunter

Director, Defense-Industrial Initiatives Group, and

Senior Fellow, International Security Program

Center for Strategic and International Studies (CSIS)

December 2, 2014

2118 RHOB

Chairman Forbes, Ranking Member McIntyre, thank you for the opportunity to testify today on the Department of Defense's offset strategy and its implications for the role of maritime and air power. It is an honor to appear as a witness before this committee, my former professional home, and a place where the critical national security questions of our time have, and I believe always will, get the thorough review they require.

The topic of today's hearing is an important one. The Department of Defense's recently announced Defense Innovation Initiative, which is tasked to develop and support a new offset strategy, is in my view a serious effort to achieve an important strategic objective. That objective is to leverage innovation, both operational and technological, to extend the Department's military advantage over potential adversaries even as those adversaries engage in carefully planned, aggressive, and increasingly successful efforts to erode that advantage. It is my view that at the most essential level, innovation is the key to the next US offset strategy. The 2012 Defense Strategic Guidance (DSG) makes this point clear, but the question of whether the US has a concrete plan to realize this objective has persisted since its release. This is the task that I believe the new Defense Innovation Initiative must tackle and the task that the Congress must ensure the Department is resourced and organized to pursue. I'll first propose how I recommend the Congress think about and assess the offset strategy, then discuss some possible approaches to such a strategy and their implications for maritime and air power, and finally I'll lay out some potential challenges that stand in the way of the next offset strategy and how Congress can help address them.

Lessons of Previous Offset Strategies

As was recently noted by Department of Defense officials when announcing the Defense Innovation Initiative, two previous offset strategies were pursed by the United States in the post-World War II era. First, President Eisenhower sought to offset the Warsaw Pact's significant numerical advantage in conventional forces in the 1950s by investing in a substantial nuclear arsenal. Later, as it became increasingly clear that the US nuclear advantage had eroded and that the nuclear arsenal did not provide the United States with the strategic flexibility required to confront the full range of security challenges posed by the Cold War, the United States adopted another offset strategy by investing in capabilities for communications, stealth, and precision guidance that yielded the technological edge that US forces have enjoyed until the present day.

A number of key lessons from the last offset strategy are highly relevant today. One overarching lesson was the need to link the offset strategy with the larger whole of government national security strategy. The successful offset strategy of the 1970s was designed to enable the larger shift in the US strategy toward more flexible response options to address Soviet aggression. The purpose of that offset strategy was to give the Commander–in–Chief conventional options for countering the Soviet ability to mass conventional forces at the high-end of conflict and to address Soviet aggression in proxy battles at the low-end. A second key lesson is how the maximization of US forces' qualitative advantage through communications, stealth, and precision guidance leveraged existing US assets. It did not require a wholesale replacement of US equipment, and capitalized on ongoing developments in commercial technology. It enabled new operational concepts, such as AirLand Battle, by spreading innovative capabilities such as precision guided munitions throughout the force, and was less about radical new weapon designs or revolutionary new platforms with the notable exception of stealth. Third, the adoption of the new offset strategy did not immediately render the nuclear arsenal, the cornerstone of the previous offset strategy, obsolete. The US continued to maintain and enhance its nuclear arsenal although the increasing accuracy of conventional weapons eventually allowed for significant decreases in the size of the nuclear arsenal.

These lessons are directly applicable to the next offset strategy and point to several ways that Congress should assess the Defense Innovation Initiative. It is critical that the use of innovation as an offset strategy is integrated within a broader national strategy. Only in a broad strategic context can it be determined which capabilities, and therefore which innovative concepts and technologies, merit enhanced investment. The 2012 DSG, the 2014 Quadrennial Defense Review, and ultimately the National Security Strategy must provide this strategic context. These documents specify a remarkably wide range of missions US forces will need to be able to perform in the future and cite the need for new capabilities in the critical domains of cyber and space. To address this diverse mission set, the next offset strategy will have to focus on capabilities with a broad array of applications. As such it is my view that the next offset strategy should consist of a set of targeted capabilities enabling new operational concepts and paired with a technology investment roadmap. The next offset strategy should not focus on platform specific investments. To be effective, the next offset strategy needs to guide investments by the Department of Defense as well as those of industry, so that the Department's investments are fully leveraged. Communication with industry therefore, including to the maximum extent possible non-traditional suppliers, will be a key enabler as will be the ability to harvest commercial technologies. The capabilities targeted in the next offset strategy must be applicable to the broadest range of threats from the high-end to the low-end of conflict. In addition, the strategy must be flexible enough to allow adjustments based on unexpected or unforeseen adversary capabilities. Lastly, the development of a new offset strategy should not imply that existing capabilities and concepts are necessarily obsolete. There will inevitably be necessary trade-offs between developing new capabilities and operational concepts and maintaining existing ones. However, we must take care not to throw the baby out with the bathwater.

The Next Offset Strategy

I do not claim to be able to lay out a fully developed offset strategy for you today that meets all the requirements I've described so far. Developing such an approach will take time and will entail a much broader discussion with the Department of Defense, the national security community, and industry. The wargaming and experimentation that the Department of Defense has indicated will be part of the Defense Innovation Initiative is a critical element in this effort. However, my expectation is that the next offset strategy will resemble the prior offset strategy more than that strategy resembled its predecessor. While the challenges of the next few decades are unlikely to be similar to those posed by the massed forces of the Warsaw Pact, many of the capabilities developed as part of the last offset strategy are likely to be highly relevant when addressing future challenges. I believe that future adversaries are likely to pursue cost-imposing strategies that seek to raise the economic and military stakes for US military action to levels they believe will be unacceptable to the American public. The US must pursue capabilities that enable effective responses at acceptable costs.

I'll illustrate a few potential approaches to the problem for the Committee to consider. A key element in the current US technological advantage comes from battlespace awareness, a detailed knowledge of the locations of friend and foe on the battlefield. Further advancing the gains in battlespace awareness achieved in the last three decades will be a critical enabler in both high-end conflicts involving advanced anti-access area denial threats and in low-end conflicts involving less technologically sophisticated, but no less deadly, threats to US forces. Given the rapid pace of development in areas such as data mining, sensor fusion, and image processing, significant advances in battlespace awareness are likely to become available in coming years. Such advances can significantly enable the ability of US forces to plan and execute successful missions against the full range of potential adversaries.

Today the need to task, process, exploit, and disseminate vast quantities of data generated by a wide range of battlefield sensors is a significant driver of both cost and personnel, and is a major limiting factor to increased battlespace awareness. Technological advances that automate data processing while leveraging the unique capabilities of the human brain can pay large dividends in capacity and ultimately capability. Likewise, the ability to transmit growing volumes of data across a networked force by efficiently utilizing, and where necessary increasing, bandwidth will be vitally important. Teaming of manned and unmanned assets has the potential to significantly extend the capability of existing high value manned platforms at reduced cost and risk. Finally, the ability of US forces to act cooperatively with partner forces can provide access to additional sensors and information that enhance our battlespace awareness while significantly complicating potential adversaries' ability to impose costs on the United States.

Equally important to extending US capabilities for battlespace awareness will be denying adversaries' battlespace awareness. Stealth and electronic warfare have been and will remain significant contributors in this area even as cyber takes on an increasingly important role. Advances in both hardware and software should enable significantly increased sophistication in our ability to degrade adversaries' battlespace awareness. While by no means exhaustive, this list gives some indication of areas where investments in innovation and new operational concepts, leveraging the rapid pace of developments in commercial technology, are likely to pay significant dividends.

Application to the Role of Maritime and Air Power

The capabilities described above readily lend themselves to application in the realm of maritime and air power. Capabilities such as the Airborne Warning and Control System (AWACS) and the Combined Engagement Capability (CEC) were pioneered by the Air Force and Navy respectively and were designed to provide exactly the kind of networked battlespace awareness that is likely to be key to both sides in future conflicts. The United States Marine Corps Distributed Operations concept applied a related conceptual approach to the control of terrain in Iraq and Afghanistan while the Army, working with the Joint IED Defeat Organization, developed integrated sensor networks for the protection of US forward operating bases. There is significant opportunity to further extend these networked approaches to missions such as air defense; command, control, communications, and intelligence; precision strike; suppression of enemy air defense; force protection; and a broad range of other ground, maritime and air missions. Perhaps more importantly, there is abundant opportunity to degrade adversaries' ability to utilize these same networked approaches. Such counterforce applications drew little focus from the US when we possessed a virtual monopoly on advanced battlespace awareness. An increased focus on battlespace awareness capabilities only reinforces the importance of the space and cyber domains to maritime and air operations as these domains represent vital links for developing battlespace awareness.

Enabling Innovation

Support for the funding and flexibility needed for the Department to adopt innovative approaches is far and away the most important role Congress can play in the development of the next offset strategy. For those who may hesitate to support such an approach due to doubts about whether an organization as large and bureaucratic as the Department of Defense is capable of the necessary innovation, you must consider the evidence of the past 10 years of war. During this period, the Department has been able to innovate to quickly address threats posed by a range of determined and adaptive enemies. The Department responded rapidly to well over 500 validated joint urgent operational needs and a much greater number of service specific urgent requirements to prevent loss of life and the potential for mission failure. In so doing, the Department was able to leverage innovation, both in industry and within its own labs and commands, to address a range of serious threats including Improvised Explosive Devices (IEDs) and indirect fires. Through the dedicated effort of thousands of individuals working to rapidly field innovative solutions to Iraq, Afghanistan and other parts of the globe, and with the strong support of Congress for these efforts, thousands of military men and women are alive today. This innovation was accomplished using many of the tools, contracting approaches, and personnel employed in the existing acquisition system but utilized in a highly tailored, expedited way. The essential ingredients that enabled these successes were senior leadership focus, up to and including the Secretary of Defense, a clear and rapid process for validating urgent requirements, and financial flexibility. While the approach to addressing urgent operational needs cannot simply be replicated to produce an offset strategy, I believe the recent demonstrations of the US military's capacity for innovation makes clear that innovation is alive and well if the Department and Congress take the steps necessary to enable it.

Challenges to Innovation

Unfortunately, it is not a foregone conclusion that the Department will be able to retain the capacity for innovation against low-end threats demonstrated in the last 10 years let alone retool that capacity for addressing high-end threats that frequently require longer development efforts to counter. Investments in innovation compete for resources with other priorities with strong constituencies. In an era of declining budgets, it is all too easy to decrement investments in innovation in order to pay readiness bills created by sequestration or to pay bills resulting from the failure to make needed changes in force structure or compensation. The temptation to short change investment in innovation to finance daily operations is not unlike the trade-off made by those using pay day lenders to borrow against tomorrow's paycheck to cover today's expenses, and it holds great risk for national security over the medium to long term.

This risk is by no means simply theoretical. Recent research by the Center for Strategic and International Studies on defense contract trends documents that contract spending for research and development (R&D) dropped by 21% in fiscal year 2013, the first year of sequestration, significantly more than the overall 10% drop in the defense budget under sequestration and the 16% drop in all contract spending. Although fiscal year 2014 contract data is not yet fully available, initial indications are that the Department experienced another decline in R&D contract spending in the past fiscal year, albeit less dramatic. This data is unsurprising given the known reductions in R&D budget accounts due to sequestration, but it is important confirmation because not all funding in R&D budget accounts pays directly for actual research and development. Furthermore, R&D contracts can sometimes utilize funding from other budget accounts. It is increasingly clear that the threat to innovation in our current budget environment is very real, and it will require senior leadership attention of the sort contemplated in the Defense Innovation Initiative to address. It will also require the active support of Congress to ensure that innovation is enabled and not stifled by dynamics both internal to and external to the Department of Defense, most especially sequestration.

Reducing Barriers to Innovation

A significant opportunity for Congress to facilitate the next offset strategy comes from reducing barriers to the adoption of innovative approaches. Such approaches require relatively open communication with industry and careful tailoring of the acquisition process. Rapid acquisition processes are appropriate where technologies are mature and operational needs compelling, however, many innovative approaches will require longer term acquisition approaches. Modular open system approaches can be utilized in the vast majority of systems to enable the rapid incorporation of innovative capabilities throughout system lifecycles. Most critically, Congress can support easier access to commercial technologies. Existing statutory requirements such as the Truth in Negotiations Act (TINA) and the Cost Accounting Standards (CAS) were designed to protect the government's interest in acquiring technology from firms that engage in both government and non-government work. In that sense these statutory requirements address issues in the government-industry relationship that are highly relevant today and going forward, however, the implementation mechanisms for these systems date largely from the 1970s and are not well aligned with modern commercial practices. A careful review of TINA and CAS implementation could substantially enhance the Department of Defense's ability to access the cutting of technology.

Importance of Congressional Support

In closing, I commend the Committee's decision to focus on the Department of Defense's next offset strategy at this hearing and recommend that the Committee continue to follow this effort closely. I've tried to suggest how the Committee can assess the Department's progress in developing the next offset strategy and to indicate several areas where congressional action can contribute positively to its development and implementation. Congressional support for change is likely to prove decisive to success.

CSIS | CENTER FOR STRATEGIC & INTERNATIONAL STUDIES

Published on Center for Strategic and International Studies

Andrew Philip Hunter

Andrew Hunter is a senior fellow in the International Security Program and director of the Defense-Industrial Initiatives Group at CSIS. He focuses on issues affecting the industrial base, including emerging technologies, sequestration, acquisition policy, and industrial policy. From 2011 to November 2014, Mr. Hunter served as a senior executive in the Department of Defense (DOD). Appointed as director of the Joint Rapid Acquisition Cell in 2013, his duties included fielding solutions to urgent operational needs and leading the work of the Warfighter Senior Integration Group to ensure timely action on critical issues of warfighter support. From 2011 to 2012, he served as chief of staff to Ashton B. Carter and Frank Kendall, while each was serving as under secretary of defense for acquisition, technology, and logistics. Additional duties while at DOD include providing support to the Deputy's Management Action Group and leading a team examining ways to reshape acquisition statutes.

From 2005 to 2011, Mr. Hunter served as a professional staff member of the House Armed Services Committee, leading the committee's policy staff and managing a portfolio focused on acquisition policy, the defense industrial base, technology transfers, and export controls. From 1994 to 2005, he served in a variety of staff positions in the House of Representatives, including as appropriations associate for Representative Norman D. Dicks, as military legislative assistant and legislative director for Representative John M. Spratt Jr., and as a staff member for the Select Committee on U.S. National Security and Military/Commercial Concerns with the People's Republic of China. Mr. Hunter holds an M.A. degree in applied economics from the Johns Hopkins University and a B.A. degree in social studies from Harvard University.

DISCLOSURE FORM FOR WITNESSES
CONCERNING FEDERAL CONTRACT AND GRANT INFORMATION

INSTRUCTION TO WITNESSES: Rule 11, clause 2(g)(5), of the Rules of the U.S. House of Representatives for the 113th Congress requires nongovernmental witnesses appearing before House committees to include in their written statements a curriculum vitae and a disclosure of the amount and source of any federal contracts or grants (including subcontracts and subgrants) received during the current and two previous fiscal years either by the witness or by an entity represented by the witness. This form is intended to assist witnesses appearing before the House Committee on Armed Services in complying with the House rule. Please note that a copy of these statements, with appropriate redactions to protect the witness's personal privacy (including home address and phone number) will be made publicly available in electronic form not later than one day after the witness's appearance before the committee.

Witness name: Andrew Hunter
Capacity in which appearing: (check one)

X_ Individual

____Representative

If appearing in a representative capacity, name of the company, association or other entity being represented:

FISCAL YEAR 2014

federal grant(s) / contracts	federal agency	dollar value	subject(s) of contract or grant
Fixed-Price Contracts	DoD	$119,996	
Defense Products	DoD	$119,939	
Defense Components	DoD	$119,933	
Defense Competition	DoD	$119,693	

FISCAL YEAR 2013

federal grant(s) / contracts	federal agency	dollar value	subject(s) of contract or grant
The Future of the National Guard	DoD	$94,997	
Process-Leading Innovation Case Study	DoD	$198,752	

FISCAL YEAR 2012

Federal grant(s) / contracts	federal agency	dollar value	subject(s) of contract or grant
Identifying Governance Best Practices in System of Systems	NPS - Grant	$98,221	
Cost for DOD Sourcing	NPS - Grant	$119,512	

Federal Contract Information: If you or the entity you represent before the Committee on Armed Services has contracts (including subcontracts) with the federal government, please provide the following information:

Number of contracts (including subcontracts) with the federal government:

   Current fiscal year (2014):_____;
   Fiscal year 2013:_____;
   Fiscal year 2012:_____.

Federal agencies with which federal contracts are held:

   Current fiscal year (2014):_____;
   Fiscal year 2013:_____;
   Fiscal year 2012:_____.

List of subjects of federal contract(s) (for example, ship construction, aircraft parts manufacturing, software design, force structure consultant, architecture & engineering services, etc.):

   Current fiscal year (2014):_____;
   Fiscal year 2013:_____;
   Fiscal year 2012:_____.

Aggregate dollar value of federal contracts held:

Current fiscal year (2014):_____;
Fiscal year 2013:_____;
Fiscal year 2012:_____.

Federal Grant Information: If you or the entity you represent before the Committee on Armed Services has grants (including subgrants) with the federal government, please provide the following information:

Number of grants (including subgrants) with the federal government:

Current fiscal year (2014):_____;
Fiscal year 2013:_____;
Fiscal year 2012:_____.

Federal agencies with which federal grants are held:

Current fiscal year (2014):_____;
Fiscal year 2013:_____;
Fiscal year 2012:_____.

List of subjects of federal grants(s) (for example, materials research, sociological study, software design, etc.):

Current fiscal year (2014):_____;
Fiscal year 2013:_____;
Fiscal year 2012:_____.

Aggregate dollar value of federal grants held:

Current fiscal year (2014):_____;
Fiscal year 2013:_____;
Fiscal year 2012:_____.

The Role of Maritime and Air Power in DoD's Third Offset Strategy

David Ochmanek

RAND Office of External Affairs

CT-420

December 2014

Testimony presented before the House Armed Services Committee, Subcommittee on Seapower and Projection Forces on December 2, 2014

David Ochmanek[1]
The RAND Corporation

The Role of Maritime and Air Power in DoD's Third Offset Strategy[2]

Before the Committee on Armed Services
Subcommittee on Seapower and Projection Forces
United States House of Representatives

December 2, 2014

The Department of Defense (DoD) has embarked on a new initiative—the Third Offset Strategy—in order to "sustain and advance America's military dominance for the 21st century." The initiative is necessitated in part by the fact that "DoD no longer holds exclusive access to some of the most cutting-edge technology the way [it] once did." For this reason, DoD will intensify its efforts to "explore and develop new operational concepts, and new approaches to warfighting, war-gaming and professional military education."[3]

This initiative, and the resources required to make it a reality, are urgently needed. As the Chairman of the Joint Chiefs of Staff, General Martin Dempsey observed in DoD's report of the 2014 Quadrennial Defense Review, he expects

> . . . the risk of interstate conflict in East Asia to rise, the vulnerability of our platforms and basing to increase, our technology edge to erode, instability to persist in the Middle East, and threats posed by violent extremist organizations to endure. Nearly any potential future conflict will occur on a much faster pace and on a more technically challenging battlefield. And, in the case of U.S. involvement in conflicts overseas, the homeland will no longer be a sanctuary either for our forces or for our citizens.[4]

Present trends, in short, are not favorable. Of particular concern for future U.S. power projection operations is the accelerating proliferation of systems and concepts aimed at impeding U.S. forces' access to key regions in Eurasia and dramatically raising the risks and suppressing the

---

[1] The opinions and conclusions expressed in this testimony are the author's alone and should not be interpreted as representing those of RAND or any of the sponsors of its research. This product is part of the RAND Corporation testimony series. RAND testimonies record testimony presented by RAND associates to federal, state, or local legislative committees; government-appointed commissions and panels; and private review and oversight bodies. The RAND Corporation is a nonprofit research organization providing objective analysis and effective solutions that address the challenges facing the public and private sectors around the world. RAND's publications do not necessarily reflect the opinions of its research clients and sponsors.
[2] This testimony is available for free download at http://www.rand.org/pubs/testimonies/CT420.html.
[3] Secretary of Defense Chuck Hagel, "A New Era for the Defense Department," *Defense One*, November 18, 2014.
[4] Note that this was written prior to Russia's recent aggression against Ukraine and the takeover by the so-called Islamic State of large areas od Syria and Iraq. U.S. Department of Defense, Quadrennial Defense Review 2014, p. 61.

operating tempo of those forces that do deploy forward. Key elements of these anti-access/area denial (A2/AD) strategies are: accurate ballistic and cruise missiles; dense, integrated surface-to-air defenses; large numbers of modern 4th generation fighter aircraft and capable air-to-air missiles; near-real time surveillance and reconnaissance systems; hardened, redundant command and control networks; electronic warfare (jamming) systems; anti-satellite weapons; and cyber weapons. Today, China is, by far, the leading exponent of sophisticated A2/AD capabilities, while Russia has also been able to field substantial numbers of these systems. As such, China will be the "pacing threat" motivating the modernization of U.S. forces and capabilities for power projection. [5]

States, such as North Korea and Iran, that cannot afford large numbers of these sophisticated systems are fielding them selectively and in smaller numbers. North Korea has also been developing and testing nuclear weapons and delivery systems. When deployed in deeply buried facilities or on mobile launchers, even a small nuclear arsenal can be difficult to neutralize, posing serious risks of escalation. North Korea and Iran also espouse military doctrines that incorporate irregular forces and unconventional operations as means of countering U.S. conventional superiority.

The other factor threatening the future of U.S. power projection capabilities is the growth of constraints on U.S. defense spending due to the budget deficit and other demands on the federal budget. Defense appropriations in Fiscal Years 2012 and 2013 were, respectively, 6 percent and 13 percent less than that for which the Department of Defense (DoD) had been planning. [6] These cuts have been imposed against the Pentagon's "base budget," meaning that they have come on top of reductions in spending for combat operations in Iraq and Afghanistan. Moreover, these cuts have been absorbed by a force that is, in some ways, less well trained and equipped than it was in 2001. Neither the Air Force nor the Marine Corps, for example, has been able to invest heavily in new combat aircraft, resulting in a force that is the oldest in history. In the case of the Air Force, the average age of the aircraft in its fleet now exceeds 26 years. [7]

---

[5] For a broad assessment of these developments and their potential significance, see David Shlapak, *Question of Balance: The Shifting Cross-Strait Balance and Implications for the U.S.*, CT-343, RAND, 2010. See also, Office of the Secretary of Defense, *Military and Security Developments Involving the People's Republic of China 2014*, U.S. Department of Defense; and Evan Braden Montgomery, "Contested Primacy in the Western Pacific: China's Rise and the Future of U.S. Power Projection, *International Security*, Spring 2014, pp. 115-149."

[6] Office of the Secretary of Defense (Comptroller)/Chief Financial Officer, *United States Department of Defense Budget Request Overviews* for Fiscal Years 2011, 2012, and 2013.

[7] As CSBA's Todd Harrison has observed, during the buildup associated with the wars in Iraq and Afghanistan, "Rather than getting larger and more expensive, . . . the military has become smaller, older, and more expensive." Todd Harrison, *Chaos and Uncertainty: The FY2014 Defense Budget and Beyond*, Center for Strategic and Budgetary Assessments, October 2013. See also http://www.defenseindustrydaily.com/aging-array-of-american-aircraft-attracting-attention-0901/.

Assessing A2/AD Threats

How might a large-scale conflict with a capable adversary unfold in the 2020 time frame? And what sorts of capabilities will be called for if U.S. forces are to prevail in such a conflict?

Long-Range, Accurate Missiles. The most obvious source of concern for U.S. planners in such a scenario is the large number of accurate ballistic and cruise missiles that the adversary might field.[8] Accuracy is a key factor. The Scud missiles that Iraqi forces fired at U.S. and coalition forces in the 1991 Gulf War featured circular errors probable (CEPs) on the order of 1000 meters. This meant that those missiles could be used to harass operations by forward-based forces at fixed installations, such as airbases, but that they were unlikely to do significant damage.[9] Today, just as U.S. forces use modern, lightweight inertial measuring units, positioning data from satellites such as the Global Positioning System (GPS) constellation, and sometimes, terminal homing sensors to guide weapons to their targets, so do some adversaries.[10] These technologies can allow an adversary to achieve much higher accuracies (on the order of 20-30 meters or less for some models), meaning that missiles with ranges of 1000 kilometers or more can attack not only specific installations but particular facilities on those installations with high probabilities of damage.[11] As a result, forward-based forces, such as combat and support aircraft, can now be vulnerable to being damaged on the ground before they get to the fight. And supplies and facilities needed to support combat operations, such as fuel, munitions, maintenance hangars, runways, crew quarters, and communications sites may be vulnerable as well. China has also reportedly developed ballistic and cruise missiles that can detect and attack large ships at sea, raising the risks to aircraft carriers, large surface combatants, and other naval components of U.S. power projection forces.[12]

U.S. and allied forces are investing in active defense systems, such as Patriot, THAAD, and sea-based SM-3 missiles, to shoot down ballistic and cruise missiles. However, the defensive systems are expensive, they take time to deploy to the theater, and, thus far, have not consistently achieved high probabilities of kill against the most capable threat systems. As a consequence, they can be overwhelmed by large salvo attacks and taken out of the fight.

---

[8] For example, DoD estimates that in 2013 China possessed more than 1000 short-range ballistic missiles (SRBMs) capable of reaching Taiwan. The PLA is also deploying growing numbers of conventionally armed medium-range ballistic missiles, as well as sea-launched and air-launched land attack cruise missiles. *Military and Security Developments Involving the People's Republic of China 2014*, pp. 6- 9.
[9] For an early and seminal assessment of the potential for conventionally armed missiles to threaten operations at forward airbases, see John Stillion and David T. Orletsky, *Airbase Vulnerability to Conventional Cruise- and Ballistic Missile Attacks: Technology, Scenarios, and U.S. Air Force Responses*, MR-1208-AF, RAND, 1999.
[10] *Military and Security Developments Involving the People's Republic of China 2014*, p. 40.
[11] Shlapak et al, pp. 32-35.
[12] *Military and Security Developments Involving the People's Republic of China 2014*, pp. 7, 31, 36.

Integrated Air Defense Systems (IADS). Radar-guided surface-to-air missiles (SAMs) and their associated surveillance and control networks have been a feature of modern military operations since the 1960s. Since the Gulf War, U.S. forces have demonstrated the ability to suppress, avoid, and degrade these defenses through a combination of dynamic targeting, specialized radar-homing weapons, electronic jamming, stealth aircraft, and other measures. These techniques have been instrumental in allowing U.S. and coalition air forces to operate within the enemy's airspace largely unimpeded.

Beginning in the late 1990s, first Russia, then China began investing in a new generation of SAMs that feature powerful tracking and guidance radars equipped with electronic counter-measures and high-performance missiles capable of engaging fighter aircraft at ranges of 125 miles or more. The radars and missile launchers are mounted on mobile vehicles that make them difficult to locate and target.[13] When fielded in sufficiently dense arrays and supported by survivable command and control facilities, it can be difficult, dangerous, and time consuming to suppress these modern IADS.

Fighter Aircraft. Russia and China complement their surface-based air defenses with substantial numbers of highly capable fighter aircraft, such as the Russian-made Su-27. Roughly comparable in range, payload, and aerodynamic capabilities to the formidable U.S. F-15C fighter, these aircraft can operate over areas not well covered by SAMs, threatening both combat aircraft (fighters and bombers) and support assets, such as aerial refueling and surveillance aircraft. Equipped with modern air-to-air missiles and backed by robust networks for command and control, Russian and Chinese fighters today represent a more formidable challenge to air superiority than any adversary the United States has faced since World War II.

To date, neither Russia nor China has fielded an operational 5th generation fighter, such as the U.S. F-22 or F-35. In a direct engagement, assuming aircrews with comparable skills, 5th generation fighters would be expected to achieve highly favorable exchange ratios against their 4th generation foes. But only a small portion of the U.S. fighter force to date has been equipped with 5th generation aircraft and Russia and China are both building their own advanced fighters.[14] Moreover, Russian and Chinese commanders would strive to limit the flow of U.S. combat aircraft

---

[13] http://www.globalsecurity.org/military/world/russia/s-300pmu2.htm.

[14] China has flown prototypes of the J-20 advanced fighter, which has been characterized as a "4.5 generation" aircraft. Today, the United States fields 120 5th generation F-22 fighters in operational units out of a total force of approximately 2,700 Air Force, Navy, and Marine Corps front-line fighters. See Bill Sweetman, "J-20 Stealth Fighter Design Balances Speed and Agility, *Aviation Week and Space Technology*, November 3, 2014. See also Government Accounting Office, *Tactical Aircraft: DoD's Ability to Meet Requirements is Uncertain, with Key Analyses Needed to Inform Upcoming Investment Decisions*, GAO-10-789, July 2010, p. 4 (figures adjusted to reflect only combat coded aircraft).

into the theater and into the fight through heavy attacks on their forward operating bases. It is therefore possible that in a conflict involving either of these states U.S. and allied air forces would have to fight outnumbered, at least in the conflict's early phases.[15]

These developments will make it much more costly for the United States and its allies to gain the air superiority to which they have grown accustomed. In a future conflict air superiority could be contested for days or weeks and achieved only after incurring potentially significant losses.[16]

The Struggle for Information Superiority. Adversaries that have studied U.S. military campaigns since Operation Desert Storm understand the critical role that information superiority plays in modern military operations. In that conflict and others since then against conventional foes, U.S. forces have been able to develop a "common operating picture" (COP) of the battlefield, providing commanders and front-line units with current information about the location and status of both enemy and friendly units. The picture is built by fusing information from myriad sources, including airborne and space-based sensors, human intelligence, and reports from friendly units. The picture is not perfectly accurate or entirely comprehensive, of course, but U.S. commanders today have far better situational awareness of a large and complex battle space than commanders at any time in history. Importantly, they have also been able to degrade the enemy's COP.

Potential adversaries are striving to develop similar capabilities, fielding sensor systems on satellites, unmanned aerial vehicles, and other airborne sensor platforms; building command centers where the information from these sensors is fused; and using multiple communication systems to connect these nodes and units in the field. They are also working to degrade the quality, timeliness, and reliability of the COP available to U.S. forces. China, for instance, has fielded large numbers of electronic jamming systems to degrade U.S. theater communications.[17] China's forces also have capabilities to interfere with the sensors on surveillance satellites and to destroy the satellites themselves.[18] And numerous adversaries are using cyber operations to attempt to penetrate U.S. military information networks in order to both extract information and to disrupt operations. As a result, U.S. forces cannot be confident that, in a conflict with the most capable adversaries, they would have an accurate and timely view of the battlefield or that they could communicate effectively at all times in the theater.

---

[15] Shlapak et al, p. 67.
[16] Shlapak et al, p. 118.
[17] J. Randy Forbes, "Caucus Brief: Chinese Military Capable of Jamming U.S. Communications System," The Congressional China Caucus, September 20, 2013, http://forbes.house.gov/news/documentsingle.aspx?DocumentID=350448.
[18] Wendell Minnick, "China Developing Capability to Kill Satellites, Experts Say," *Defense News*, August 4, 2014.

Undersea Warfare. The PLA Navy is building modern submarines, including nuclear-powered vessels, and equipping them with capable weapon systems, including long-range anti-ship and land attack cruise missiles. And while DoD judges that the PLA Navy's deep-water anti-submarine warfare capability "seems to lag behind its air and surface warfare capabilities," it notes that China "is working to overcome shortcomings in this and other areas."[19]

In short, the loss of the near-monopoly that U.S. forces have enjoyed over a wide range of key capabilities can have potentially profound effects on their ability to project power and to defend U.S. interests, allies, and partners. Analyses of future conflicts against the most capable adversary forces in the 2020 time frame and beyond suggest that U.S. and allied forces will have to fight for advantages that they have heretofore taken almost for granted. *Without very substantial investments in new capabilities and concepts for power projection, U.S. and allied decision makers could lose confidence in the United States' ability and will to defeat aggression.* Should this happen, our role as security partner of choice would be called into question, and our influence and ability to help sustain a stable and economically vibrant world order would erode. DoD's Third Offset initiative or something very much like it is, therefore, needed if U.S. forces are to acquire the capabilities and develop the new operating concepts called for to meet this stressing set of challenges.

Meeting the Challenge: Developing New Military Concepts and Capabilities

If U.S., allied, and partner forces are to retain credible capabilities to deter and defeat an adversary with advanced military capabilities, new investments in platforms, weapons, infrastructure, and support systems will be called for. But meeting the challenge will require more than simply buying and fielding new and better gear. The scope of the A2/AD challenge posed by the most capable adversaries also calls for new concepts for the conduct of power projection operations. Money, time, and talent must therefore be allocated not only to the development and procurement of new equipment and infrastructure but also to concept development, gaming and analysis, field experimentation, and exploratory joint force exercises.

The following key capability areas merit priority attention:

- **Enhanced capabilities to thwart the enemy's attacking forces early in a conflict**. Adversaries intend to use their A2/AD capabilities to create a window of opportunity during which they can achieve their operational objectives. In response, the United

---

[19] *Military and Security Developments Involving the People's Republic of China 2014*, pp. 31-32.

States and its allies must find more ways to damage and destroy the adversary's attacking forces and suppress their key supporting assets—his operational centers of gravity—early in a conflict; i.e., prior to gaining air and maritime superiority in proximity to adversary territory and forces.[20] This is key. Because U.S. forces have for so long been confident in their ability to dominate these domains in conflicts against less capable adversaries, they have not, for the most part, invested in capabilities for ISR and strike in contested environments. This is not a "first strike" capability; it is about defeating those forces that the adversary is using to attack a U.S. ally or partner or U.S. forces and bases.

- **Resilient basing** – Making forward-deployed forces and bases (including surface ships) more survivable (see below).

- **Rapid suppression/destruction of enemy air defenses**, including jamming of radars, disrupting command and control, destroying missiles on their launchers, and neutralizing large formations of fighter aircraft.

- **Degrading the enemy's situational awareness** and control capabilities while enhancing the resiliency of ours.

- **Cyber defense and offense** - Making the information networks used by U.S. forces less vulnerable to cyber attacks and at the same time developing improved tools for degrading the networks of adversary forces.

It is beyond the scope of this statement to identify specific programs, systems, or technology areas most appropriate for providing these capabilities. However, some broad implications are clear:

- **The United States should continue to modernize its fleets of both long-range and shorter-range military aircraft.** One reaction to the growth of adversary strike capabilities has been to seek ways to conduct more joint operations from bases

---

[20] The key term here is *operational* centers of gravity. Successful defense will require that U.S. and allied forces be able to quickly damage and destroy the forces that the adversary is using to prosecute aggression. If they can do that it will not be necessary or desirable to threaten to impose additional costs through escalatory attacks, either vertical (i.e., against political or economic centers of gravity) or horizontal (i.e., against military forces far outside of the contested area). As the United States develops new capabilities, concepts, and postures for countering A2/AD threats, it should make clear through its public statements and its military exercises that it does not intend such escalation, in order to minimize prospects for a destabilizing dynamic.

beyond the range of the most numerous threats (e.g., short- and medium-range ballistic missiles and air-launched cruise missiles). This makes sense to some degree and bombers, long-range air- and sea-launched cruise missiles, aerial refueling aircraft, and long-range, long-dwell ISR platforms will play important roles in any future U.S. CONOPs for power projection. But high-performance shorter-range systems (i.e., 5th generation fighter aircraft) will also be needed in order to defend against enemy bomber raids and contest for freedom of maneuver in contested battle space (e.g., over the Taiwan Strait). The likelihood that U.S. air forces will have to fight outnumbered for some time underscores the need for fighter aircraft and air-to-air weapons that are qualitatively superior to those of the most capable potential adversary states.

- **Larger stocks of advanced weapons and munitions are called for**. A conflict with an advanced A2/AD adversary will consume large quantities of missiles and precision guided munitions. Early on, weapons such as anti-ship and land-attack cruise missiles that make possible attacks on key targets from ranges beyond the reach of the adversary's most capable air defense systems will be in high demand. And because U.S. forces will be encountering far larger arrays of advanced fighter aircraft and SAMs than in previous conflicts, they will expend large numbers of air-to-air and air-to-surface missiles. Such weapons are costly but are essential to getting the most capability out of a force that is sortie-limited.

- **New approaches are required for basing and operating forward forces**. During the Cold War, airbase survivability was provided at forward bases primarily by hardening key facilities, such as aircraft hangars, maintenance structures, weapons storage, and crew quarters. With the advent of highly accurate ballistic and cruise missiles, broader-based approaches are essential. Efforts should include: (1) hardening selected facilities in theaters threatened by missile and air attacks, (2) ensuring that land-based forces can operate from a large number of austere facilities, (3) investing in more capabilities for rapid repair of damaged facilities, especially runways, (4) confusing enemy targeting of both land bases and surface ships through camouflage, decoys, and deception measures, and (5) providing better protection of key facilities through active defenses against ballistic and cruise missiles. The last of these approaches is particularly challenging given the high cost, modest effectiveness, and vulnerability of theater ballistic missile defense systems. Efforts are underway to develop lower-cost ways of intercepting ballistic missiles and these should receive high priority. In the near term, identifying new airfields that U.S. forces might use in wartime, making modest improvements to the infrastructure at those airfields where feasible, developing capabilities and procedures for operations at unimproved airfields, and conducting exercises at such fields could contribute greatly to reducing the vulnerability of U.S. forces in wartime while strengthening deterrence. This calls for developing relationships with new partners and deepening existing ones. In addition, more dispersed and expeditionary basing will place new burdens on joint logistics, base security, and engineering assets.

- **U.S. assets based in space will need to be made more robust**. Much of the outcome of the fight for information superiority will turn on the extent to which one side or the other can maintain such critically important capabilities as over-the-horizon communications, surveillance, and positioning, many of which are on satellites. Many adversaries have or are developing weapons that can jam or otherwise interfere with the operations of these satellites. And Russia and China have anti-satellite missiles that can destroy satellites, at least in low-earth orbit. Countering these threats will call for enhanced space situational awareness systems, which monitor activities in space and characterize and track objects there. These efforts will need to be complemented by a host of measures to make satellite constellations less vulnerable.[21] Policy makers should also consider the potential benefits and costs of developing airborne and terrestrial complements to selected space-based capabilities and fielding offensive space capabilities, as a means of both deterring attacks on U.S. assets and degrading adversaries' C4ISR.

Of course, countering the threats posed by potential adversary states is not solely a problem for the United States. In fact, it would be unwise and infeasible for the United States to attempt to address these challenges unilaterally. Allies and partners, particularly those directly or indirectly threatened by adversary activities or in the same region, have a strong interest in ensuring that their forces can impose a high price on an aggressor and contribute effectively to combined regional operations that may be led by the United States.

With these goals in mind, the proliferation of systems and technologies that are causing U.S. planners such concerns can be turned to our advantage. If allies and partners invest wisely, they can impose smaller-scale A2/AD challenges on the states that are wielding them against them.

---

[21] One promising approach is to make greater use of commercial satellites (both U.S. and foreign-owned and operated). DoD can make direct use of imaging and communications satellites, for example. It can also put its own payloads on satellites launched primarily for other customers. Doing so complicates the adversary's targeting problem. See U.S. Department of Defense and Office of the Director of National Intelligence, *National Security Space Strategy: Unclassified Summary*, January 2011, pp. 9 – 11.

Taiwan, for example, has both the economic means and the technical and operational savvy to develop, deploy, and operate systems such as short-range UAS and anti-ship cruise missiles, shallow water mines, rocket artillery, mobile short-range air defenses, and communications jamming gear, all of which, properly employed, could contribute mightily to an effective defense against invasion.[22] Similar capabilities could also help states such as the Philippines and Vietnam, which have faced coercive threats from China over control of disputed territories in the South China Sea, to better monitor and protect areas close to their shores.

GCC (Gulf Cooperation Council) countries concerned about aggression from Iran likewise could invest in hardened airbases, mine-sweeping craft, missile defenses, UAS, and other capabilities useful in countering conventional and unconventional threats. And through regular combined forces exercises and planning and more inter-operable communications networks, the United States, its allies, and partners can make the whole of their capabilities as great as the sum of their parts. But make no mistake: enhancements such as these cannot take the place of U.S. forces and the commitment to use them as the means of offsetting major imbalances in military power.

Ingredients for Success

If the Third Offset Strategy—or any serious force planning effort undertaken in this challenging environment—is to succeed, the following elements will be essential:

- Deliberations and decisions about resource allocation must be underpinned by rigorous and credible joint analysis of future operational challenges and potential solutions to them. Specifically, DoD will need to reconstitute and reinvigorate its ability to conduct iterative, carefully adjudicated tabletop exercises and model-based campaign assessments in order to identify key gaps in programmed capabilities, test nascent operational concepts for power projection, and evaluate candidate systems to enable those concepts.

- More resources will be needed for modernizing elements of the force and supporting new operational concepts. Many practical, proven ways of addressing key A2/AD threats are left unfunded or underfunded today because of budget constraints. If the limits on DoD's topline imposed by the Budget Control Act are not lifted in FY 2016 and beyond, it is very

[22] See Michael Lostumbo, *A New Taiwan Strategy to Adapt to PLA Precision Strike Capabilities*, RAND and The Institute for National Security Studies, 2011, pp. 7-10.

difficult to see how even a flawlessly executed Third Offset approach could be sufficient to meet growing challenges.

- Congress must partner with the Administration to allow greater flexibility and agility in managing defense programs and resources. As Secretary Hagel has observed, DoD needs "flexibility to undertake critical cost-saving measures, from reducing excess basing to reforming military compensation to shedding outdated platforms and systems."[23]

Conclusion

Assessing trends in the military balance between the United States and China or other potential adversaries, some observers have concluded that the competition is becoming too demanding and that efforts to maintain America's status as the security partner of choice for many of the world's most important states are economically unaffordable, operationally infeasible, or both. Some counsel a "strategic retrenchment" and adoption of a strategy of "offshore balancing," under which the United States would disengage from its major security commitments and rely on "regional power balances to contain rising powers."[24] Others claim that the United States can deter adventurism, coercion, and aggression by China and other adversaries "on the cheap" by threatening to impose economic costs in response to aggression and/or by building up the self-defense capabilities of regional allies and partners.[25]

The problem with these approaches, put bluntly, is that they are not likely to work. They can be valuable complementary approaches to a strategy aimed at denying Chinese forces their objectives, but by themselves such indirect approaches are not likely to deter or defeat a determined China or other powerful state. Gaming and analysis of hypothetical conflicts involving China and neighboring states in the 2020 time frame suggest that in plausible scenarios, if the goal is to defeat a large Chinese military operation, there is simply no substitute for the type of and level of military support that the United States uniquely can provide. And this support must be brought to bear quickly and be sustained throughout the campaign.

The most credible deterrent to aggression is one that presents the adversary with the prospect of failure: He perceives that his forces will be unlikely to achieve the operational objectives assigned

---

[23] Hagel, "A New Era for the Defense Department," p. 3.

[24] Christopher Layne, "America's Middle East Grand Strategy After Iraq: The Moment for Offshore Balancing Has Arrived," *Review of International Studies*, January 2009, p. 10.

[25] For a discussion of the merits of a "war of economic attrition," see T.X. Hammes, "Offshore Control: A Proposed Strategy for an Unlikely Conflict," *Strategic Forum*, National Defense University, June 2012. For an assessment of the potential of allies and partners to enhance their self-defense capabilities, see David Gompert and Terrence Kelly, "Escalation Clause: How the Pentagon's New Strategy Could Trigger War With China," *Foreign Policy*, August 2, 2013.

to them due to a combination of the capabilities of the defending forces and will to employ them. Posturing forces to support such a robust direct defense or denial strategy can be difficult for a nation that is called upon to project power over long distances. But future U.S. forces, properly modernized, postured, and employed in concert with the forces of regional allies and partners, should be capable of posing very significant obstacles to aggression by potential adversary states. This is not to imply that doing so will necessarily be easy or inexpensive, but the costs of a credible defense posture are worth the security advantages it provides. This, as I understand it, is the prime motivation behind DoD's Third Offset initiative. It is a worthy and, I believe, achievable objective.

David Ochmanek

David Ochmanek is a senior defense analyst at RAND. From 2009 until 2014 he was the Deputy Assistant Secretary of Defense for Force Development. Prior to joining the Office of the Secretary of Defense, he was a senior defense analyst and director of the Strategy and Doctrine Program for Project Air Force at the RAND Corporation, where he worked from 1985 until 1993, and again from 1995 until 2009. From 1993 until 1995, he served as Deputy Assistant Secretary of Defense for Strategy. Prior to joining RAND, Ochmanek was a member of the Foreign Service of the United States, serving from 1980 to 1985. From 1973 to 1978, he was an officer in the United States Air Force. He is a graduate of the United States Air Force Academy and Princeton University's Woodrow Wilson School of Public and International Affairs. He has been an adjunct professor at Georgetown and George Washington Universities.

DISCLOSURE FORM FOR WITNESSES
CONCERNING FEDERAL CONTRACT AND GRANT INFORMATION

INSTRUCTION TO WITNESSES: Rule 11, clause 2(g)(5), of the Rules of the U.S. House of Representatives for the 113th Congress requires nongovernmental witnesses appearing before House committees to include in their written statements a curriculum vitae and a disclosure of the amount and source of any federal contracts or grants (including subcontracts and subgrants) received during the current and two previous fiscal years either by the witness or by an entity represented by the witness. This form is intended to assist witnesses appearing before the House Committee on Armed Services in complying with the House rule. Please note that a copy of these statements, with appropriate redactions to protect the witness's personal privacy (including home address and phone number) will be made publicly available in electronic form not later than one day after the witness's appearance before the committee.

Witness name: David Ochmanek

Capacity in which appearing: (check one)

___Individual

_X_Representative

If appearing in a representative capacity, name of the company, association or other entity being represented:

FISCAL YEAR 2014

federal grant(s) / contracts	federal agency	dollar value	subject(s) of contract or grant
1	DoD	$63,759,733	NDRI

FISCAL YEAR 2013

federal grant(s) / contracts	federal agency	dollar value	subject(s) of contract or grant
1	DoD	$63,539,233	NDRI

FISCAL YEAR 2012

Federal grant(s) / contracts	federal agency	dollar value	subject(s) of contract or grant
1	DoD	$63,920,538	NDRI

Federal Contract Information: If you or the entity you represent before the Committee on Armed Services has contracts (including subcontracts) with the federal government, please provide the following information:

Number of contracts (including subcontracts) with the federal government:

        Current fiscal year (2014):_1_____;
        Fiscal year 2013:_1_____;
        Fiscal year 2012:_1_____.

Federal agencies with which federal contracts are held:

        Current fiscal year (2014):_see attached_____;
        Fiscal year 2013:_see attached_____;
        Fiscal year 2012:_see attached_____.

List of subjects of federal contract(s) (for example, ship construction, aircraft parts manufacturing, software design, force structure consultant, architecture & engineering services, etc.):

        Current fiscal year (2014):_see attached_____;
        Fiscal year 2013:_see attached_____;
        Fiscal year 2012:__see attached_____.

Aggregate dollar value of federal contracts held:

        Current fiscal year (2014):_$63,759,733_____;
        Fiscal year 2013:_$63,539,233_____;
        Fiscal year 2012:_$63,920,538_____.

Federal Grant Information: If you or the entity you represent before the Committee on Armed Services has grants (including subgrants) with the federal government, please provide the following information:

Number of grants (including subgrants) with the federal government:

        Current fiscal year (2014):_0_____;
        Fiscal year 2013:__0_____;
        Fiscal year 2012:__0_____.

Federal agencies with which federal grants are held:

        Current fiscal year (2014):_N/A_____;
        Fiscal year 2013:__N/A_____;
        Fiscal year 2012:__N/A_____.

List of subjects of federal grants(s) (for example, materials research, sociological study, software design, etc.):

        Current fiscal year (2014):_N/A_____;
        Fiscal year 2013:_N/A_____;
        Fiscal year 2012:_N/A_____.

Aggregate dollar value of federal grants held:

        Current fiscal year (2014):_0_____;
        Fiscal year 2013:_0_____;
        Fiscal year 2012:_0_____.

This testimony was done under the auspices of RAND's National Defense Research Institute (NDRI).

Federal agencies with which federal contracts are held:

The RAND Corporation is an independent, non-profit organization that performs research and analysis. During the time period in question (FY2012 through FY2014), RAND has had contracts and grants with various agencies of the federal government to perform research and analysis. Research has been performed for the Departments of Agriculture, Commerce, Defense, Education, Energy, Health and Human Services, Homeland Security, Justice, Treasury, Veterans Affairs, the Administrative Office of the United States Courts, the Centers for Disease Control and Prevention, the National Institutes of Health, the Environmental Protection Agency, the Federal Communications Commission, the Federal Reserve Banks of Boston and New York, the Intelligence Community, the Medicare Payment Advisory Commission, the National Aeronautics and Space Administration, the National Science Foundation, the Social Security Administration, and the U.S.-China Economic and Security Review Commission. RAND has contracts with the Department of Defense to operate three federally funded research and development centers (FFRDC): PROJECT AIR FORCE for the U.S. Air Force; Arroyo Center for the U.S. Army; and National Defense Research Institute for the Department of Defense.

List of subjects of federal contract(s) (for example, ship construction, aircraft parts manufacturing, software design, force structure consultant, architecture & engineering services, etc.):

The National Defense Research Institute (NDRI), a federally funded research and development center (FFRDC), conducts a broad range of analysis for the Office of the Secretary of Defense (OSD), the Joint Staff, the Unified Combatant Commands, the defense agencies, the United States Marine Corps, and the United States Navy.

www.ingramcontent.com/pod-product-compliance
Lightning Source LLC
Chambersburg PA
CBHW081133290526
45795CB00006B/2217